W9-BIV-412

INVESTING IN OUR CHILDREN

BUSINESS AND THE PUBLIC SCHOOLS

A Statement by the Research and
Policy Committee of the
Committee for Economic Development

WITHDRAWN
STCCC LIBRARY
4601 Mid Rivers Mall Drive
St. Peters, MO 63376

Library of Congress Cataloging in Publication Data

Committee for Economic Development. Research and
    Policy Committee.
    Investing in our children.

    "1985"
    1. Industry and education—United States.
    2. High school graduates—Employment—United States.
    3. Education—Economic aspects—United States.
    4. Teachers—Salaries, pensions, etc.—United States.
    5. Public schools—United States. I. Title.
    LC1085.C66   1985   371'.01'0973   85-15189
    ISBN   0-87186-780-X
    ISBN   0-87186-080-5 (pbk.)

First printing in bound-book form: 1985
Paperback: $9.50
Library binding: $11.50
Printed in the United States of America
Design: Stead Young & Rowe Inc
Photographs: Cover and Chapters 1 and 4, Alan S. Orling,
    photographs of Hunter College Campus School.
    Chapters 2, 3, and 5, Los Angeles Education Partnership.

COMMITTEE FOR ECONOMIC DEVELOPMENT
477 Madison Avenue, New York, N.Y. 10022
(212) 688-2063
1700 K Street, N.W., Washington, D.C. 20006
(202) 296-5860

CONTENTS

INVESTING IN OUR CHILDREN

BUSINESS AND THE PUBLIC SCHOOLS

RESPONSIBILITY FOR CED STATEMENTS ON NATIONAL POLICY

The Committee for Economic Development is an independent research and educational organization of two hundred business executives and educators. CED is nonprofit, nonpartisan, and nonpolitical. Its purpose is to propose policies that will help to bring about steady economic growth at high employment and reasonably stable prices, increase productivity and living standards, provide greater and more equal opportunity for every citizen, and improve the quality of life for all. A more complete description of CED appears on page 107.

All CED policy recommendations must have the approval of trustees on the Research and Policy Committee. This committee is directed under the bylaws to "initiate studies into the principles of business policy and of public policy which will foster the full contribution by industry and commerce to the attainment and maintenance" of the objectives stated above. The bylaws emphasize that "all research is to be thoroughly objective in character, and the approach in each instance is to be from the standpoint of the general welfare and not from that of any special political or economic group." The committee is aided by a Research Advisory Board of leading social scientists and by a small permanent professional staff.

The Research and Policy Committee does not attempt to pass judgment on any pending specific legislative proposals; its purpose is to urge careful consideration of the objectives set forth in this statement and of the best means of accomplishing those objectives.

Each statement is preceded by extensive discussions, meetings, and exchange of memoranda. The research is undertaken by a subcommittee, assisted by advisors chosen for their competence in the field under study. The members and advisors of the subcommittee that prepared this statement are listed on page x.

The full Research and Policy Committee participates in the drafting of recommendations. Likewise, the trustees on the drafting subcommittee vote to approve or disapprove a policy statement, and they share with the Research and Policy Committee the privilege of submitting individual comments for publication, as noted on pages 101 through 104 of this statement.

Except for the members of the Research and Policy Committee and the responsible subcommittee, the recommendations presented herein are not necessarily endorsed by other trustees or by the advisors, contributors, staff members, or others associated with CED.

RESEARCH AND POLICY COMMITTEE

Chairman
WILLIAM F. MAY

Vice Chairmen
WILLIAM S. EDGERLY/*Education and Social and Urban Development*
RODERICK M. HILLS/*Government*
JAMES W. McKEE, JR./*International Economic Studies*
ROCCO C. SICILIANO/*National Economy*

*ROY L. ASH
Los Angeles, California

RALPH E. BAILEY, Chairman and Chief
  Executive Officer
Conoco Inc.

WARREN L. BATTS, President
Dart & Kraft, Inc.

JACK F. BENNETT, Senior Vice President
Exxon Corporation

THEODORE A. BURTIS, Chairman of the
  Board
Sun Company, Inc.

OWEN B. BUTLER, Chairman of the
  Board
The Procter & Gamble Company

FLETCHER L. BYROM, Retired Chairman
Koppers Company, Inc.

ROBERT J. CARLSON, Chairman,
  President and Chief Executive
  Officer
BMC Inc.

RAFAEL CARRION, JR., Chairman of the
  Board
Banco Popular de Puerto Rico

JOHN B. CAVE, Executive Vice President–
  Finance
McGraw-Hill, Inc.

ROBERT A. CHARPIE, President
Cabot Corporation

ROBERT CIZIK, Chairman and President
Cooper Industries, Inc.

EMILIO G. COLLADO, Executive
  Chairman
International Planning Corporation

D. RONALD DANIEL, Managing Director
McKinsey & Company, Inc.

RONALD R. DAVENPORT, Chairman of
  the Board
Sheridan Broadcasting Corporation

PETER A. DEROW, President
CBS/Publishing Group

FRANK P. DOYLE, Senior Vice President
General Electric Company

W. D. EBERLE, President
Manchester Associates, Ltd.

WILLIAM S. EDGERLY, Chairman of the
  Board and President
State Street Bank and Trust Company

*THOMAS J. EYERMAN, Partner
Skidmore, Owings & Merrill

JOHN H. FILER, Former Chairman
Aetna Life and Casualty Company

EDMUND B. FITZGERALD, Chairman
  and Chief Executive Officer
Northern Telecom Limited

ROBERT E. FRAZER, Chairman
The Dayton Power and Light Company

*DONALD E. GUINN, Chairman and
  Chief Executive Officer
Pacific Telesis Group

RICHARD W. HANSELMAN,
  Chairman, President and Chief
  Executive Officer
Genesco Inc.

PHILIP M. HAWLEY, Chairman of the
  Board
Carter Hawley Hale Stores, Inc.

RODERICK M. HILLS, Of Counsel
Latham, Watkins & Hills

ROBERT C. HOLLAND, President
Committee for Economic Development

LEON C. HOLT, JR., Vice Chairman
  and Chief Administrative Officer
Air Products and Chemicals, Inc.

JAMES L. KETELSEN, Chairman and
  Chief Executive Officer
Tenneco Inc.

CHARLES M. KITTRELL, Executive
  Vice President
Phillips Petroleum Company

PHILIP M. KLUTZNICK, Senior Partner
Klutznick Investments

RALPH LAZARUS, Chairman,
  Executive Committee
Federated Department Stores, Inc.

*FRANKLIN A. LINDSAY, Chairman
Engenics, Inc.

HOWARD M. LOVE, Chairman and
  Chief Executive Officer
National Intergroup, Inc.

*ROBERT W. LUNDEEN, Chairman
  of the Board
The Dow Chemical Company

WILLIAM F. MAY, President
Statue of Liberty — Ellis Island
  Foundation, Inc.

ALONZO L. McDONALD, Chairman
  and Chief Executive Officer
Avenir Group, Inc.

JAMES W. McKEE, JR., Chairman
CPC International Inc.

ROBERT E. MERCER, Chairman of the
  Board
The Goodyear Tire & Rubber Company

RUBEN F. METTLER, Chairman of the
  Board and Chief Executive Officer
TRW Inc.

STEVEN MULLER, President
The Johns Hopkins University

NORMA PACE, Senior Vice President
American Paper Institute

VICTOR H. PALMIERI, Chairman
Victor Palmieri and Company
  Incorporated

CHARLES W. PARRY, Chairman and Chief
  Executive Officer
Aluminum Company of America

DEAN P. PHYPERS, Senior Vice President
IBM Corporation

LELAND S. PRUSSIA, Chairman of the
  Board
Bank of America N.T. & S.A.

JAMES Q. RIORDAN, Senior
  Vice President
Mobil Corporation

FRANCIS C. ROONEY, JR., Chairman of
  the Board
Melville Corporation

HENRY B. SCHACHT, Chairman of the
  Board and Chief Executive Officer
Cummins Engine Company, Inc.

DONNA E. SHALALA, President
Hunter College

PHILIP L. SMITH, President and Chief
  Operating Officer
General Foods Corporation

RICHARD M. SMITH, Vice Chairman
Bethlehem Steel Corporation

*ROGER B. SMITH, Chairman
General Motors Corporation

ELMER B. STAATS, Former Comptroller
  General of the United States
Washington, D.C.

WILLIAM C. STOLK
Easton, Connecticut

ANTHONY P. TERRACCIANO, Vice
  Chairman, Global Banking
The Chase Manhattan Bank, N.A.

WALTER N. THAYER, Chairman
Whitney Communications Company

W. BRUCE THOMAS, Vice Chairman of
  Administration and Chief Financial Officer
United States Steel Corporation

SIDNEY J. WEINBERG, JR., Partner
Goldman, Sachs & Co.

ALTON W. WHITEHOUSE, JR., Chairman
The Standard Oil Company (Ohio)

RICHARD D. WOOD, Chairman of the
  Board
Eli Lilly and Company

WILLIAM S. WOODSIDE, Chairman
American Can Company

*Voted to approve the policy statement but submitted memoranda of comment, reservation, or dissent.

SUBCOMMITTEE ON BUSINESS AND THE SCHOOLS

Chairman
OWEN B. BUTLER
Chairman of the Board
The Procter & Gamble Company

Vice Chairmen
RONALD R. DAVENPORT
Chairman of the Board
Sheridan Broadcasting Corporation

RALPH LAZARUS
Chairman, Executive Committee
Federated Department Stores, Inc.

JAMES W. McKEE, JR.
Chairman
CPC International Inc.

DONNA E. SHALALA
President
Hunter College

ALFRED BRITTAIN III
Chairman of the Board
Bankers Trust Company

ROBERT A. CHARPIE
President
Cabot Corporation

W. GRAHAM CLAYTOR, JR.
Chairman and President
Amtrak

PETER A. DEROW
President
CBS/Publishing Group

DONALD J. DONAHUE
Retired Chairman
KMI Continental Inc.

FRANCIS E. FERGUSON
Retired Chairman of the Board
Northwestern Mutual Life Insurance
Company

WILLIAM S. FISHMAN
Chairman, Executive Committee
ARA Services, Inc.

DONALD E. GARRETSON
Community Service Executive
Program
3M Company

BARBARA B. HAUPTFUHRER
Corporate Director
Huntingdon Valley, Pennsylvania

ARTHUR HAUSPURG
Chairman of the Board
Consolidated Edison Company of
New York, Inc.

CHARLES KELLER, JR.
New Orleans, Louisiana

DONALD P. KELLY
President
Kelly Briggs & Associates, Inc.

CHARLES M. KITTRELL
Executive Vice President
Phillips Petroleum Company

[1]ROBERT W. LUNDEEN
Chairman of the Board
The Dow Chemical Company

STEVEN MULLER
President
The Johns Hopkins University

[1]ALFRED C. NEAL
Harrison, New York

BARBARA W. NEWELL
Chancellor
State University System of Florida

VICTOR H. PALMIERI
Chairman
Victor Palmieri and Company
Incorporated

DEAN P. PHYPERS
Senior Vice President
IBM Corporation

S. DONLEY RITCHEY
Chairman
Lucky Stores, Inc.

BRUCE M. ROCKWELL
Chairman of the Board
Colorado National Bank

DONALD M. STEWART
President
Spelman College

J. PAUL STICHT
Chairman, Executive Committee
R. J. Reynolds Industries, Inc.

HOWARD R. SWEARER
President
Brown University

WALTER N. THAYER
Chairman
Whitney Communications Company

CHARLES C. TILLINGHAST, JR.
Providence, Rhode Island

THOMAS A. VANDERSLICE
President and Chief Executive Officer
Apollo Computer Inc.

CLIFTON R. WHARTON, JR.
Chancellor
State University of New York

WILLIAM S. WOODSIDE
Chairman
American Can Company

*Nontrustee Members**

JOHN BRADEMAS
President
New York University

W. M. MARCUSSEN
Vice President and Assistant to the
President
Atlantic Richfield Company

MARTIN MEYERSON
President Emeritus
University of Pennsylvania

VINCENT REED
Vice President/Communications
The Washington Post

[1]Voted to approve the policy statement but submitted memoranda of comment, reservation, or dissent.
*Nontrustee members take part in all discussions of the statement but do not vote on it.

ADVISORS

PAUL E. BARTON
Assessment Policy Committee
Liaison
National Assessment of
Educational Progress

DAVID BERGHOLZ
President
Public Education Fund

ALAN K. CAMPBELL
Vice Chairman
ARA Services, Inc.

ALONZO A. CRIM
Superintendent
Atlanta Public Schools

HAROLD HOWE II
Senior Lecturer
Harvard Graduate School of
Education

MICHAEL W. KIRST
Professor of Education
Stanford University

DANIEL H. SAKS
Professor of Education Policy and of
Economics
Institute for Public Policy Studies
Vanderbilt University

FRANK W. SCHIFF
Vice President and Chief Economist
Committee for Economic Development

NATHANIEL M. SEMPLE
Vice President and Secretary, Research
and Policy Committee
Committee for Economic Development

ALBERT SHANKER
President
American Federation of Teachers

P. MICHAEL TIMPANE
President, Teachers College
Columbia University

PROJECT DIRECTORS

DENIS P. DOYLE
Resident Fellow in Education
American Enterprise Institute for Public
 Policy Research
MARSHA LEVINE
Education Consultant
American Enterprise Institute for Public
 Policy Research

PROJECT EDITOR

SANDRA KESSLER HAMBURG
Assistant Director of Information
Committee for Economic Development

PROJECT STAFF

SUZANNE L. DIDIER
Administrative Assistant
Committee for Economic Development
MARGARET M. EVANS
Administrative Assistant
Committee for Economic Development
RUTH MUNSON
Conference Manager
Committee for Economic Development

STAFF COUNSELOR

SOL HURWITZ
Senior Vice President
Committee for Economic Development

TASK FORCE ON THE TEACHING PROFESSION

Chairman
ALAN K. CAMPBELL
Vice Chairman
ARA Services, Inc.

Members
REX D. ADAMS
Vice President, Employee Relations
Mobil Oil Corporation
J. MYRON ATKIN
Dean, School of Education
Stanford University
MARK M. BIELER
Vice President
Bankers Trust Company
DEAN C. CORRIGAN
Dean, College of Education
Texas A & M University
R. BYARD HIRES
Senior Vice President
Paine Webber Jackson & Curtis Inc.
HAROLD HOWE II
Senior Lecturer
Harvard Graduate School of Education
JAMES A. KELLY
President
Spring Hill Center
JUDE RICH
Partner
McKinsey & Company
ALBERT SHANKER
President
American Federation of Teachers

ANITA SUMMERS
Chairman, Department of Public Policy and
 Management
Wharton School, University of Pennsylvania
P. MICHAEL TIMPANE
President, Teachers College
Columbia University

Director

MARSHA LEVINE
Education Consultant
American Enterprise Institute for Public
 Policy Research

Staff

DENIS P. DOYLE
Resident Fellow in Education
American Enterprise Institute for Public
 Policy Research
SOL HURWITZ
Senior Vice President
Committee for Economic Development
NATHANIEL M. SEMPLE
Vice President and Secretary, Research and
 Policy Committee
Committee for Economic Development

PURPOSE OF THIS STATEMENT

This nation was built on a foundation of local initiative and individual diversity. Therefore the strategy for education reform we present in this statement is based on the common-sense view that real and meaningful changes can only occur where learning takes place — in the school building, in the classroom, and in the relationship between student and teacher.

It is not the purpose of this statement to trace the decline of our nation's schools, nor to dwell on past failures. Rather, our goal is to find new ways to provide *all* of our children with the opportunity to learn, to grow, and to become informed and productive adults.

The Committee for Economic Development has a long-standing commitment to improving the quality of our schools. For many years it urged the business community to take an active role in this endeavor. CED's first major policy statement on education, the 1959 report *Paying for Better Public Schools,* stated clearly that business has "a responsibility, as citizens, to participate in the local, state, and national effort to improve the schools." The report also asserted that "we need better schools and we can have them. The essential requirement is that we should want them strongly enough."

More than twenty-five years later, our society must once again face up to the challenge of restoring the nation's public schools. We must want change badly enough to work vigorously for improvement. We believe that implementing the recommendations we make in this statement can help the schools improve significantly, increasing public education's contribution to society and its value to our children.

THE COSTS OF FAILURE

Three years ago, a study of our nation's flagging competitiveness motivated CED to undertake this study. We became convinced that one important reason for our growing inability to compete in world markets was the inadequacy of our education system. An initial survey of our trustees revealed that many employers believed the schools were graduating too many students who lacked even the basic requirements for success in the workplace.

Although the economic benefits of quality education and the cost of educational failure are key concerns of this report, we are also aware of the crucial role education plays in providing every child equality of opportunity. Of course, the public schools cannot and should not supplant the family or the community in building character or instilling the values of a free society. Nevertheless, all of us have an obligation to provide our children and our children's children with the best possible public education. We have a responsibility to see that our schools develop the intellectual skills and reinforce the positive attitudes and behavior that will serve our children well.

STRATEGY FOR REFORM

As a business organization, the Committee decided to focus its study on those key educational issues on which we could offer a unique expertise. Consequently, we targeted our efforts on four issues where our special perspective could contribute to innovative and lasting reform.

■ **Employability.** We identified the intellectual and behavioral traits that are most important for success in the work force and in higher education.

■ **Educational Investment.** We offered strategies for increasing the nation's investment in education that would have the greatest payoff both for students and for society.

■ **Teachers and Schools.** We developed a program for upgrading the professionalism of the nation's teachers and improving the quality of educational management.

■ **Business/School Collaboration.** We examined how schools and businesses can forge effective partnerships.

The needs of education reform are sweeping. Therefore, this report does not deal in depth with such critical issues as the role of technology in education's future. We do, however, strongly endorse the need for expanded education research and data collection in these and other areas and better application of research findings.

What I find most remarkable and most challenging about this CED statement is its powerful call for systematic and coordinated reform in key areas of education. And I am heartened by its recognition of the important contribution business can make to education reform — how business can work with the schools both nationally and locally to develop workable reforms and to implement them in a coherent and consistent manner.

A FOUNDATION OF RESEARCH

We are grateful for the many excellent studies and reports on education reform that have been issued in recent years. The reports by the National Commission on Excellence in Education, the Education Commission of the States, and others have helped heighten public awareness of the critical need for improved public education.

Although the findings and recommendations of many of these reports have been of great value in developing a background and context for our study, we have also conducted extensive research of our own. On page 106 is a listing of papers prepared for the CED Subcommittee on Business and the Schools by a group of eminent education experts. These papers will be published by CED in a separate volume, and we are indebted to the experience and scholarship of those who helped us in this effort.

In two issues in particular, employability and teacher quality, we saw the need for research in depth. To examine whether the schools are adequately preparing students to succeed in the work force or in higher education, we commissioned a nationwide survey of large and small businesses and four-year institutions of higher learning. The results of these surveys are reported in Chapter 2 of this statement.

Our concern for improving the quality of the teaching profession was such that we established a special task force to examine ways to improve the recruitment, training, management, motivation, and compensation of teachers. This task force was headed by Alan K. Campbell, vice chairman of ARA Services, Inc. A list of the members appears on page xi.

ACKNOWLEDGEMENTS

Very deep thanks go to the chairman of this subcommittee, Owen B. Butler, chairman of the board of The Procter & Gamble Company. Brad Butler's humanity and vision were the guiding force for this project, and the strength of this document is due largely to his insightful leadership. We are also grateful to the outstanding business leaders and education experts who worked so diligently on this subcommittee. Their names are listed on page x.

We are also grateful for the knowledge, experience, and effort brought to this study by the project directors, Denis P. Doyle and Marsha Levine of the American Enterprise Institute for Public Policy Research. Special thanks also go to staff counselor Sol Hurwitz and to project editor Sandra Kessler Hamburg.

In addition, we would like to acknowledge the important financial and intellectual contribution made by the foundations, listed on page 105, that have so generously supported this project.

William F. May
Chairman
Research and Policy Committee

CHAPTER 1

INTRODUCTION AND SUMMARY OF RECOMMENDATIONS

The most important investment this nation can make is in its children. Although many institutions influence our children's education and development — the family, the community, the church, the media — the focus of this policy statement is on the institution in which the public plays a direct and dominant role: America's public schools.

When public schools are successful, they become a national treasure. They can instruct and inspire our young people. They can give life to local communities, contributing to their economic growth and social well-being. They can pave the road to employment, greater opportunity, and more productive lives. In our pluralistic democracy, the schools can forge a common culture while respecting diversity.

But for all these possibilities, many of our schools stand accused of failing the nation's children and leaving the economy vulnerable to better-educated and more highly trained international competitors.*

As business executives and educators, we are keenly aware of education's role in producing informed and productive citizens. We also see increasing evidence that education has a direct impact on employment, productivity, and growth and on the nation's ability to compete in the world economy. Therefore, we cannot fail to respond to the following warning signs:

■ Employers in both large and small businesses decry the lack of preparation for work among the nation's high school graduates. Too many students lack reading, writing, and mathematical skills, positive attitudes toward work, and appropriate behavior on the job. Nor have they learned how to learn, how to solve problems, make decisions, or set priorities. Many high school graduates are virtually unemployable, even at today's minimum wage.

■ Well over one-quarter of the nation's youth never finish high school. Many who graduate and go on to higher education need remedial reading and writing courses, which about two-thirds of U.S. colleges now provide.

■ Nearly 13 percent of all seventeen-year-olds still enrolled in school are functionally illiterate and 44 percent are marginally literate. Among students who drop out, an estimated 60 percent are functionally illiterate.

In contrast, Japan, America's most important economic competitor, has the highest rate of high school completion and literacy in the world, close to 100 percent. Japanese students study more and learn more. They spend more time in class than their American counterparts do; and by the time they graduate from high school, they have completed the equivalent of the second year at a good American college. In science and mathematics, Japanese test scores lead the world.

Japanese schools do not restrict themselves to technical training and rote learning. Japanese children are taught to appreciate the value of hard work and self-discipline; of teamwork as well as competition.

We recognize that the mission and purpose of our public schools go far beyond the preparation of young people for employment. Our schools should prepare our children to exercise the rights and obligations of citizen-

---

*See memorandum by ALFRED C. NEAL (page 101).

TEN IMPERATIVES FOR THE SCHOOLS

The reform strategy embodied in this policy statement can be characterized by the following ten imperatives for guiding the public schools:

1. Educational priorities should be better defined, and resources should be invested where the payoffs will be high. As a proportion of total spending, instruction requires a larger investment; administration and bureaucracy need less. Priority should be given to preschool programs for the disadvantaged and to programs that address the special educational needs of junior high school students.

2. Employability should not be confused with vocationalism. Employability requires problem-solving skills, command of the English language, self-discipline, and the ability to acquire and apply new knowledge.

3. The central purpose of education is to develop the potential of every student, regardless of race, sex, or physical handicap.

4. Teachers are professionals. They should be held to high standards and rewarded accordingly.

5. Parents are a critical component of successful public schools.

6. Greater trust should be placed in the initiative of individual schools. Teachers and administrators should have increased decision-making power.

7. States should refrain from excessive regulation, centralization, and control of the schools. But they should set standards, monitor achievement, and intervene if schools fail to perform.

8. A new coalition to support the public schools is needed — one that joins business, labor, and civic leaders with parents, educators, and school boards.

9. Education research and development and its effective utilization should be given greater emphasis. There is a great deal that we do not yet know about education, and much of what we do know is not being applied in the classroom.

10. Business should make a long-term commitment to support the public schools. Companies should provide policy and project support and targeted funding, with the expectation that the schools will improve their performance. But business should not be expected to provide general funding for education beyond the taxes it pays to the community.

ship. They should enhance equal opportunity and reward talent, merit, and enterprise. They should help students reach their full potential.

Nevertheless, we believe that one of the most important ways people can realize their potential is through productive and rewarding work. If our children do not have this necessary preparation for employment — if they have not developed healthy attitudes, behavior patterns, and communication and learning skills — the other very important goals of education become difficult to achieve.

The sorry state of U.S. public education has aroused the attention of educators, policy makers, and business leaders. Reform proposals issued since 1983 by the National Commission on Excellence in Education, the Education Commission of the States, and other major national, state, and local organizations have awakened the public to the serious problems confronting our nation's public education system. Activity at the state level has increased dramatically, and some 200 state committees and commissions, working under public and private auspices, are currently engaged in public school improvement. Many of these reform strategies call on the business community to take an active role in upgrading public education.

This policy statement builds on those efforts, providing a business and economic perspective on the performance of our public schools.* It offers a coordinated reform strategy that reflects our combined experience in corporate management and education.

Many of the goals embodied in this reform strategy can be met through better allocation of existing resources or through creativity, innovation, and a strong commitment to improvement. But many needed reforms, such as increased teacher salaries, more preschool education for the disadvantaged, and additional research, will cost more money. **We believe that any call for comprehensive improvement in the public schools that does not recognize the need for additional resources is destined for failure.****

We also believe that successful reform requires a concerted effort to confront the special educational needs of the lowest-achieving students — those who are at the greatest risk of dropping out or who remain in school without acquiring basic skills. We need to increase our expectations of these students and, with appropriate help, to move them toward the performance standards we expect of all our nation's students.

Although this statement centers on the elementary and secondary levels of public education, we realize that our public schools are only one key part of a continuous process of lifelong learning. Elementary and secondary education should build on the values and teaching of the home and family and provide the foundations for further education and training in postsecondary institutions and in the workplace.

---

*See memorandum by ROGER B. SMITH (page 101).

**See memorandum by ROY L. ASH (page 101).

THE CASE FOR
BUSINESS INVOLVEMENT

Human resources determine how the other resources of the nation will be developed and managed. Without a skilled, adaptable, and knowledgeable work force, neither industry nor government can work efficiently or productively.

The schools are the central public institution for the development of human resources. Tomorrow's work force is in today's classrooms; the skills that these students develop and the attitudes toward work that they acquire will help determine the performance of our businesses and the course of our society in the twenty-first century.

The case for business involvement not only centers on the benefits business derives from education, but also on what business can contribute. School management and organization can be strengthened through application of modern management techniques, and business guidance in conducting and applying research can have a major impact on this activity in the public schools. Business planning techniques can also help schools prepare better for the future as new demographic forces radically change the makeup of our student and teacher population.

A firm and enduring commitment to excellence in education on the part of America's business community is not merely a matter of philanthropy; it is enlightened self-interest. As employers, taxpayers, and responsible community members, business can regard an investment in education as one that will yield a handsome return.

SUMMARY OF CONCLUSIONS
AND RECOMMENDATIONS

The recommendations summarized here and explained in greater detail in subsequent chapters are based on a *bottom-up* strategy. This strategy is founded on the premise that reform is most needed where learning actually takes place — in the individual school, in the classroom, and in the interaction between teacher and student.

Our policy recommendations focus on four interrelated issues on which this Committee can provide a special perspective and expertise. These are discussed in the four succeeding chapters:

- Employability: Student Needs, Business Needs

- Investment Strategies in Education

- Teachers and Schools

- Business and the Schools: Shared Goals, Common Interests

Appropriate policies in these four areas can be woven into a coherent, systematic, and integrated strategy for significantly strengthening public elementary and secondary education in the United States. Although improvements can result from taking action in any one of these areas, the cumulative impact of acting simultaneously in all four can be formidable.

Businesses and schools are different in many ways, but as complex enterprises they have much in common. It is our belief that despite the special forces at work in the public sector, schools cannot improve very much unless their fundamental practices conform more with what we know to be the principles of effective organization and management.

EMPLOYABILITY: STUDENT NEEDS, BUSINESS NEEDS

Public education's most important task is to ensure that all schoolchildren are grounded in basic academic and behavioral skills.* Our school system should prepare youngsters for responsible citizenship and should impart skills and attributes that will enable them to succeed in productive employment or higher education.

Business, in general, is not interested in narrow vocationalism. It prefers a curriculum that stresses literacy and mathematical and problem-solving skills. Such a curriculum should emphasize learning how to learn and adapting to change. The schools should also teach and reward self-discipline, reliability, teamwork, acceptance of responsibility, and respect for the rights of others.

The strategies called for in this chapter include reassessment and realignment of school curricula, imposing higher expectations and more rigorous standards for student behavior and accomplishment, developing appropriate and accurate performance measures, and providing insights from business management that can assist schools in developing an organizational climate that supports improvement. A significant finding is the need for comprehensive reform of the vocational education system.

Invisible Curriculum. The signals a school transmits to students about what is and what is not acceptable behavior constitute an *invisible curriculum.* Poor work habits are often the cause of academic failure and later

---

*See memorandum by FRANKLIN A. LINDSAY (page 102).

unemployment. We urge schools and teachers to institute policies and practices that encourage development of such positive traits as self-discipline, reliability, and perseverance.

Curriculum Reform. We believe that state and local authorities ought to be primarily responsible for deciding what youngsters in their jurisdiction should learn and for developing an appropriate curriculum that balances the knowledge and skills students need to function as responsible adults with desirable local and regional variations.

We believe that all Americans need to become proficient in English. We support bilingual education as long as English mastery is the end product of the program.

Higher Standards. A high school diploma should indicate that a student has met or exceeded an established standard of achievement, and we urge all states to establish a minimum standard of performance for awarding a diploma. We also endorse honors diplomas to signify superior accomplishment.

We applaud the trend toward periodic testing for basic skills and recommend that all states and localities that have not already done so immediately adopt such programs.

It is critical that more be done to raise the performance of lower-achieving students in order to reduce the unacceptably high percentage of

---

A "BOTTOM-UP" STRATEGY

Our recommendations form a "bottom-up" strategy that views the individual school as the place for meaningful improvements in quality and productivity. This strategy does not minimize the importance of states, localities, and the federal government in defining goals, setting priorities, and providing resources. Nor does it overlook the role that the state and local authorities must play when schools and school systems fail to meet minimum standards. The states should provide "top-down" guidance and support to local schools by establishing clear goals and high standards and by developing precise measuring tools to evaluate educational achievement. At the same time, the states should give the schools maximum freedom to develop and implement the methods that would best achieve those goals.

The focus of our recommendations, therefore, is on the individual school — its students, teachers, and administrators — and the community it serves. Our central concern is with the instructional process and the interaction between student and teacher. We give careful attention to the selection, training, motivation, compensation, and working conditions of the nation's present and future classroom teachers. We also place special emphasis on improving the management of the individual school, for we see many applicable lessons from business experience in handling professional employees and utilizing resources more effectively.

---

dropouts. Higher standards need to be accompanied by greater efforts to help those who have difficulties in academic achievement.

Business Insight, Business Support. We recommend the development of a feedback mechanism through which employers can keep the schools informed about the performance of their graduates in the workplace.

Borrowing from business practice, we recommend that states exempt a fixed percentage of their especially effective schools from restrictive regulations so that these schools can be freer to design programs that best accomplish their educational objectives.

Parental Involvement. Business should develop flexible policies that encourage both parents and interested nonparents — particularly hourly employees — to participate actively in their community's schools.

Vocational Education. The term *vocational education* should be limited to those programs specifically designed to prepare students to enter a particular field upon graduation. All other forms of nonacademic instruction should be identified by a different term to avoid confusing them with programs that impart specific job skills.

We recommend that before any student is allowed to enter occupationally specific training, he or she should be required to demonstrate an adequate level of academic achievement. All vocational education majors should be expected to complete a core academic curriculum in addition to their occupationally specific training.

Area vocational centers, which centralize occupationally specific training for an area's high schools, show much promise and should be expanded where possible. Those vocational high schools and vocational programs in comprehensive high schools which exist to "warehouse" students who are not performing adequately in academic subjects should be closed. We recommend limited trial programs to test the use of contracting to private suppliers for vocational education services in the public schools.

In addition, we urge greater use of cooperative education programs which combine basic education with part-time work experiences, and we recommend that business participate in these programs.

INVESTMENT STRATEGIES IN EDUCATION

The success of education reform will depend not only on *how much* we invest in education but also on *how wisely* we invest our resources.

Many of the specific reforms we advocate in this report will require increasing our present level of investment in education. While resources at all levels of government are being constrained, we believe that increasing the nation's investment in education is essential and has the potential for very significant human and financial returns. This is particularly true for preschool programs for the disadvantaged and for improvements made at the junior high school level.

It is also imperative that strategies for investment in education reflect a concern for cost-effectiveness and demonstrate an understanding of effective resource management.

This chapter is divided into two sections. The first examines the importance of education as an investment for individuals and society and discusses where the most cost-effective investments in education are likely to be found. The second deals with how education is financed and who is responsible for decisions on allocation of resources in the public schools.

Where the Money Should Go. Many recent efforts have focused at the high school level. While much more needs to be done to improve high school performance, we believe it is critical to reach students long before what is for many the last stage of the education process.*

We are convinced that the earliest stages of educational development are where we will receive the best return on our investment in education. This means a stronger focus on the elementary schools and on well-designed preschool programs for children from disadvantaged backgrounds.

We believe that junior high and middle schools, where the foundations for poor high school performance are often laid, have not received the attention they deserve. Effective research is called for to find ways in which progress in reading, mathematics, and science made in the elementary grades is carried over into the transition years of junior high school.

Some of the most difficult educational problems are posed by low-achieving students who are at high risk of dropping out. These students often have the most to gain from what school can provide. For students on the brink of dropping out, well-designed special programs that link school and work experience can be helpful and cost-effective.

For students who have already dropped out of the education system, the Job Corps seems to provide the most cost-effective model for compensatory and remedial education. We urge that federal, state, and local authorities continue to fund an adequate Job Corps program in areas where there is a significantly high dropout rate.

Increases in long-range educational productivity are likely to come from the application of high-quality education research and data collection for which the federal government retains a major responsibility. We urge the federal government to increase the quality and relevance of its education research and data collection through the Department of Education and the organizations with which it works.

The Federal Role. In addition to its vital role in supporting high-quality education research, the federal government has assumed a long-term responsibility for meeting the special educational needs of minorities, the handicapped, and women, and it should assure that this responsibility is

---

*See memorandum by DONALD E. GUINN (page 102).

being met. But it is now time for states and localities to assume a larger role in meeting their obligations to these groups.

Local Control, State Support. We are convinced of the value of local control in American public education and of the value of making the school building the focus for change and reform. In addition, local boards of education should do a better job of identifying their priorities, budgeting for them accordingly, and performing only those tasks for which funding is available.

We believe that as they assume more of the burden of financing local schools, the states must resist the impulse to run the schools. We recommend that school governance be retained at the local level and that it not be supplanted by statewide boards of education. However, we favor state standard setting as a necessary and appropriate accompaniment to state financial control.

Although states should see that all local systems have enough money to run a satisfactory program, state finance formulas should also give local communities the authority and the incentives to raise funds and make spending decisions at the district level.

TEACHERS AND SCHOOLS

We recommend enhancing and strengthening the professional roles of teachers, increasing their ability and opportunity to exercise judgment and make decisions, raising their salaries, and upgrading their working conditions. None of these improvements can be made without strengthening school management and leadership. *In sum, we are calling for nothing less than a revolution in the role of the teacher and the management of the schools.*

Compensation. We recommend increased salaries for both entry-level and career teachers in order to attract high-quality individuals into the profession. We also support financial rewards for outstanding teacher performance and recommend that school districts experiment with alternative pay systems which could provide both annual bonus awards for outstanding teachers and incentives that link pay to performance on a group basis.

Teacher compensation systems should be flexible enough to allow districts to attract teachers in subject areas where there are critical shortages.

Career Development. Career ladders can help attract and retain high-quality teachers. Career salary structures should reflect the role of the teacher as a professional educator. They should not be based on increasing levels of administrative responsibility.

Honors, mentoring roles, public recognition, stipends for travel and study, and financial grants are important rewards for outstanding performance. We recommend that school systems provide resources to fund such rewards and incentives.

Evaluations of teacher effectiveness should encourage professional growth, development, and collegial interaction and should be separated from those evaluations that are used as a basis for contract renewal, tenure, or dismissal. We recommend that school systems develop and test different models for evaluation and that teachers play an active role in this process.

Working Conditions. The ability of schools to attract and retain qualified teachers will depend heavily on the conditions of work. We recommend that the nonprofessional responsibilities associated with teaching, such as housekeeping and clerical chores, be sharply curtailed.

Management. The leadership skills of school principals are a key ingredient in any program to improve the quality of teaching. School systems should devote more resources to the continuing education of principals in modern management and leadership techniques, and in doing so should enlist the help of business. Principals should be allowed some discretion in budgetary allocations that will permit flexibility in management at the school-building level.

The business community's experience with managing organizations is relevant to the problems of teacher quality and school effectiveness. We recommend that links be created between schools and businesses to transfer this experience.

Teacher Education. Candidates for teacher education programs should be required to meet rigorous and highly selective entrance standards. In order to avoid the shortages that higher standards would create, incentives will be needed to encourage top-ranking students to enter professional education programs. Because higher standards in teacher preparation programs can substantially upgrade the quality of new teachers, we call for a national commission to address the issue of standards and how they might be satisfied.

Prospective teachers should be required to complete an undergraduate degree with a major area of study other than education, supplemented by the courses in education that will develop professional knowledge and skills.

The teacher certification process should be flexible enough to allow individuals attracted to teaching and qualified in a subject area to complete basic certification requirements while on the job.

In most jurisdictions, salary schedules are keyed to taking coursework beyond the bachelor's degree. Too often these courses are fragmented and unfocused. We recommend that coursework taken to satisfy requirements for salary increases should be more sharply focused and pertinent to the teachers' professional responsibilities and knowledge.

BUSINESS AND THE SCHOOLS:
SHARED GOALS, COMMON INTERESTS

The business community is a legitimate part of the resurgence of interest in the public schools. Business has much to gain from improvements in the quality of schools, and it has a responsibility for helping support and maintain that quality. Business also has a role to play in supporting adequate funding for the schools.

This chapter discusses three alternatives for corporate involvement: supporting the existing system where the schools are generally healthy; fostering innovative, incremental change; and working for major structural reforms in the system.

An Appropriate Role for Business. Working together, businesses and schools must determine the appropriate goal of business involvement in each community. Each firm will have to make its own choice as to the degree of its involvement, depending on local circumstances. We believe that the business community cannot be viewed as a significant source of funding for public education beyond its important role as a taxpayer in the community. On the other hand, business dollars and involvement can contribute to education research and curriculum development, and corporate funds can be leveraged with private foundation funds to broaden opportunities for public schools.

There is little doubt that the influence and power of the business community can be persuasive in arguing the case for increased public financing of the schools. This is an appropriate role for business to play.

What Business Can Do. We urge businesses to examine the potential for improving education by working with existing organizations in the community and to take the lead in establishing new organizations if needed.

Many models exist for successful business involvement in skills and curriculum development, and interested corporations should look closely at what has been shown to work when planning their involvement. In addition, we strongly encourage more businesses to share their management expertise with the public schools.

We believe the business community needs to participate in the local policy-making process. Participation on local school boards by key managers should be encouraged and supported. Moreover, we urge business executives serving on local boards to give high priority to the bottom-up management strategies we advocate in this report.

*   *   *

The strategies and policies we have recommended cannot be put in place easily or quickly. Precisely because improving education will be a long-term process, it is critically important that we begin now. Urgent efforts are needed to increase employability, develop investment strategies that have a high payoff, revitalize the teaching profession, and establish strong and enduring partnerships between business and the public schools.

Business at the highest levels must imbed in its planning and operations an on-going commitment to excellence in public education. Our schools need a well-informed and involved business leadership all year, every year.

Lasting reform will require a continuing commitment to high standards not only from business, but from parents, students, educators, school board members, and other public officials. In exchange for meeting these high standards, the public schools can expect energetic business and public support.

CHAPTER 2

EMPLOYABILITY: STUDENT NEEDS, BUSINESS NEEDS

Our public education system has two vital functions to perform. First, it should prepare youngsters to become responsible citizens who can make informed decisions on essential personal and public issues. Second, it should impart to students those skills and attributes that will enable them to succeed in productive employment or in the pursuit of higher education.

In these goals, the interests of business and education converge dramatically. Students need to be able to qualify for good jobs when they are ready to seek them; business needs broadly educated employees who have learned how to learn and who can adapt to the changing conditions of the workplace.

The United States has a highly diversified and vigorous economy, and employment opportunities can vary greatly from sector to sector and industry to industry. Nevertheless, we believe that there is a basic set of academic skills, behavioral patterns, and attitudes toward work that form the minimum requirement for success in the work force, in postsecondary education, or in the military. It is the responsibility of the schools to help students to acquire these skills, habits, and attributes.*

As part of its study of the relationship between business and the schools, this Committee has conducted extensive research into the employment needs of both large and small businesses and into the characteristics of employability. One thing is clear from our inquiries: Business in general is not interested in narrow vocationalism. In many respects, business believes that the schools in recent years have strayed too far in that direction. For most students, employers would prefer a curriculum that stresses literacy, mathematical skills, and problem-solving skills; one that emphasizes learning how to learn and adapting to change. The schools should also teach and reward self-discipline, self-reliance, teamwork, acceptance of responsibility, and respect for the rights of others.

Some forms of vocational education have demonstrated success in preparing students for specific jobs in the modern work world, and there is an important place for them. However, we are convinced that public education's most important task is to assure that all schoolchildren are grounded in basic academic skills, behavioral patterns, and positive work habits. We believe that the mission of vocational education needs to be redefined and that the entire vocational system should be drastically overhauled.

WHAT STUDENTS NEED TO BE EMPLOYABLE

At one time, employers were fairly confident that a high school diploma meant a potential employee had acquired skills, knowledge, and behavior that would be useful in the workplace. Because of the decline in educational performance and discipline in recent decades, business can no longer assume that young people graduate from school adequately prepared to read, write, reason, calculate, communicate, or accept responsibility. Many large corporations have found it necessary to conduct in-house education and training programs in order to inculcate skills and behavior patterns not already developed in school.

We believe that it is appropriate and necessary to reassess the way in which schools prepare students to function in the work force and in life. Educators need to redesign their programs and establish and enforce reasonable standards of achievement so that a high school diploma once again has meaning and value.

An alarming number of high school graduates cannot meet entry-level job requirements. Too large a percentage are unemployable at current wage

---

*See memorandum by FRANKLIN A. LINDSAY (page 102).

rates because their skills and work habits are below the level needed for acceptable productivity on the job. Logic dictates that business will not locate, be attracted to, or be able to remain in an area where there is a poorly skilled labor pool and that jobs will be lost or will fail to be created in these areas.

Mastery of the old basics of reading, writing, and arithmetic may be sufficient for entry-level jobs, but because of the constantly changing nature of work, minimum skills are not sufficient preparation for career advancement. Schools must make a greater effort to develop higher-level skills, such as problem solving, reasoning, and learning ability. These are also the same attributes that are crucial to success in higher education.

THE CHANGING WORK ENVIRONMENT

The rapid introduction of new technologies and the continuing shift of employment away from manufacturing and towards services are having a profound and irreversible impact on the type of work that today's students will encounter when they enter the job market and on the skills they will need in order to obtain and succeed in productive employment. It is likely that as computers and robotics become increasingly pervasive production tools, the number of manufacturing jobs requiring higher-level skills will be reduced. At the same time, the variety and level of skills needed to design, sell, and service manufactured products probably will increase.

THE CHANGING WORK ENVIRONMENT
A CASE STUDY OF PROCTER & GAMBLE

An example provided by The Procter & Gamble Company offers an instructive lesson in how significantly the nature of work is changing. According to the company, employees who entered manufacturing in the past generally encountered low-skilled tasks in narrowly defined jobs. Detailed operating instructions for equipment and processes changed little over the course of the employee's work life.

Increasingly, Procter & Gamble is using a participative work system, in which employees are trained to perform a broad range of tasks, including operating and maintaining equipment and carrying out administrative functions. Frequently, they perform their own quality control inspections. Participation in goal setting, budgeting, and other processes formerly viewed as the exclusive domain of management is also expected of workers. Employees work in largely self-directed teams, and problem solving and decision making are important parts of the job.

The company provides training in many of the higher-level skills needed for these jobs. But, first, prospective employees must demonstrate strong foundations in literacy and number skills and, above all, the ability to learn.

Despite considerable uncertainty as to the actual impact of technology on future jobs, the fact remains that the more *rewarding* tasks done by people will become nonroutine, placing greater demands on workers to be able to think critically, respond to changes in the environment with reasoned judgment, communicate effectively, and take part in a continuing learning process throughout their careers. Even in the routine jobs, it is likely that these characteristics will become more necessary. At the same time, the increased importance of the individual worker and of the necessity for teamwork requires self-discipline, reliability, and interpersonal skills. But are these the skills and habits that the public schools are teaching our children? The evidence suggests that they are not.[1]

EMPLOYABILITY SKILLS

If the employment needs of business have changed, it is important for schools to know how and to what degree. In 1983 and 1984, this Committee conducted an in-depth assessment of the employment needs of industry in order to gauge the gap between expectation and reality on the part of personnel officers and managers of both large and small firms.[2] The results of this survey confirm what has long been suspected by the business community: Specific occupational skills are less crucial for entry-level employment than a generally high level of literacy, responsible attitudes toward work, the ability to communicate well, and the ability to continue to learn* (see page 18).

The survey's findings convey three strong messages:

■ First, for entry-level positions, employers are looking for young people who demonstrate a set of attitudes, abilities, and behaviors associated with a sense of responsibility, self-discipline, pride, teamwork, and enthusiasm.

■ Second, employers put a strong value on learning ability and problem-solving skills.

■ Third, employers do not think that the schools are doing a good job of developing these much-needed abilities.

The results of the CED Survey of Employer Needs should give schools a better idea of what their graduates need in order to secure entry-level jobs and to succeed in the work environment. Fundamentally, an employee must come to the workplace with the attitudes and behaviors that are asso-

1. For an interesting discussion of the changing workplace, see James J. O'Toole, *Making America Work: Productivity and Responsibility* (New York: The Continuum Publishing Company, 1981), pp. 168–183.

2. Marsha Levine, "Summary of Report: Survey of Employer Needs" an unpublished paper prepared for the Committee for Economic Development's Subcommittee on Business and the Schools, 1984. More information on this and other papers prepared for this study appears on page 106.

*See memorandum by THOMAS J. EYERMAN (page 103).

ciated with wanting to do a good job; if the employee is not responsible, dependable, and willing to learn, other abilities are of little value. Nevertheless, once these first requirements are met, problem-solving skills become paramount for advancement on the job. CED is not presuming to tell the schools what to teach or how to teach it. Nor are we suggesting that the school program should be geared entirely to the needs of the marketplace. We are equally concerned with those aspects of education that help students develop intellectually, culturally, and socially. But it is clear that the same qualities that promote success in the workplace are those that will help turn a youth into a responsible adult and an informed citizen.

CED SURVEY OF EMPLOYER NEEDS

The CED Survey of Employer Needs was sent to three different sample groups: 438 large companies, including CED's trustee companies and a randomly drawn sample of Fortune 500 companies; 6,000 small companies drawn from a random sampling of the membership of the National Federation of Independent Businesses; and 500 postsecondary institutions (which were sent a modified version of the survey). The survey questionnaires were developed after extensive consultation with the marketing and personnel development directors of The Procter & Gamble Company and with the assistance and support of AT&T; Dow Chemical Company; The J.C. Penney Company; Richardson, Bellow, Henry and Company, Inc.; Federated Department Stores; The Pillsbury Company; and Burger King (a division of Pillsbury). The resulting survey was a composite instrument reflecting the views of different sectors of industry, including manufacturing, retailing, banking, and services. The questionnaire was designed for four major categories of work: office and clerical workers, sales and service workers, technicians, and semiskilled workers. The response rate for the large companies was unusually high, 56 percent, or 244 separate companies. Because each company was sent up to four different surveys (one for each work category), a total of 678 surveys were returned from this group. The small business response was not so large, about 10 percent for a total of 646 questionnaires. Although this rate was low, the response from the CED and Fortune 500 companies was large enough to allow us to reach several important conclusions.

The survey identified sixty attributes that were grouped into ten clusters, each representing a broad attitude, skill, or behavior.

- Striving to do work well
- Priority setting and working under pressure
- Problem solving and decision making
- Working well with others
- Communicating
- Learning how to learn

We urge schools, students, parents, and employers to make effective use of the information gained from the CED Survey of Employer Needs and other sources. These findings can help schools to devise more appropriate curricula; students to make better-informed choices concerning school courses and their future pursuits in higher education and work; parents to assist their children in making these choices; and business in its support of public education and the involvement of employees in their children's schooling. Furthermore, we urge business to provide schools periodically with updated information on employability characteristics as a valuable feedback mechanism (see page 26).

- Physical and safety demands
- Number skills
- Office skills
- Mechanical and laboratory skills

Each attribute was rated on three scales: its importance for entry-level success; its importance for advancement in the workplace; and the difficulty of finding people with that attribute.

The large companies that responded to the survey ranked those characteristics having to do with "striving to do work well," "learning how to learn," "priority setting," and "communicating" as the four most important attributes associated with entry-level success. The response of small companies was similar, with "striving to do work well," "learning how to learn," "priority setting," and "working well with others" ranked most important.

When asked to identify the characteristics that contribute to advancement on the job, both groups of respondents made nearly the same choices, except that large companies were more concerned with the ability to solve problems and make decisions than with the ability to communicate. However, learning how to learn was ranked by both large and small companies as the most important attribute for getting ahead.

Finally, respondents from both groups indicated that all these attributes, particularly the ability to set priorities and to learn, were difficult to find in young applicants.

The 500 two- and four-year colleges and universities were included in the survey to test whether the characteristics associated with employment success are the same ones that college officials associate with success in college-level academics. The college officials identified the same five clusters of attributes as the large employers, with communications skills rated as most important.

These findings are confirmed by a number of sources, including a report by the National Assessment of Educational Progress (NAEP), which suggests that the area of greatest student decline is in "critical thinking skills and problem solving" (see Chapter 3, page 50).

REASSESSING AND REALIGNING THE CURRICULUM

Schools and educational authorities must clearly identify their goals and objectives and decide how to deploy available educational resources most effectively. Schools cannot be all things to all people; if they try, they will invariably fail.

THE INVISIBLE CURRICULUM

Such traits as honesty, reliability, self-discipline, cooperativeness, competitiveness, and perseverance are as important to continued scholarship and responsible citizenship as they are essential to success in the workplace. Schools have a responsibility — and an opportunity — to help instill these habits.

The signals that a school transmits to students about the importance of these traits constitute an *invisible curriculum*. If schools tolerate excessive absenteeism, truancy, tardiness, or misbehavior, we cannot expect students to meet standards of minimum performance or behavior either in school or as adults. It is not surprising that a student who is allowed to graduate with numerous unexcused absences, regular patterns of tardiness, and a history of uncompleted assignments will make a poor employee. Under these circumstances, students have no reason to believe that punctuality or timeliness are taken seriously by adults or that a failure to observe them will have adverse consequences.

Schools that develop and reinforce good habits, shared values, and high standards of behavior are most likely to produce graduates who succeed in higher education and work. **We urge schools and teachers to institute policies and practices that are specifically designed to encourage self-discipline, reliability, perseverance, and other positive traits.**

It is easy to place full blame for a decline in character development at the schoolhouse door. Far more responsible, however, are the explicit and implicit messages sent by families and by society in general.[3] But we cannot expect to tell parents how to raise their children, and society's attitudes cannot be changed easily or quickly. As citizens, one of the few institutions on which we can have a direct influence is public education.

---

3. For an interesting discussion of the decline of the work ethic in U.S. public schools and the effect on achievement, see Barbara Lerner, "American Education: How Are We Doing?," *Public Interest*, No. 69 (Fall 1982), p. 72.

A COMMON CURRICULUM

For success in the work force and in life, all students should be expected to develop a set of core academic skills. Although we strongly support local control of schools, we also believe that a common base of knowledge makes continued learning more effective and efficient and enables individuals to function best in mainstream American society. **Therefore, we believe that it is important for public schools to develop a common curriculum, one that balances the teaching of the basics of what should be mastered in a modern, technological society with the need for desirable regional or local variations.**

Although we do not advocate the development or imposition of a national curriculum, we believe that there does need to be substantial agreement at the state and local levels on what should be taught in the schools. We do not think this recommendation poses serious implementation problems for the schools or for state and local school authorities. For one thing, we do not believe that there would be great variation in what different states and different school districts think should constitute a minimum core curriculum. In addition, we stress the word *minimum*; we believe that substantial room should be left in the curriculum for local discretion. But we do believe that all children should learn to read, should master the fundamentals of written and verbal communication, should know how to compute and reason mathematically, should understand the basics of science, and should have a common knowledge of history and literature.

The most necessary element in a common curriculum is mastery of English. **We believe that all Americans must become proficient in the English language in order to work and live in the modern world.** The issue is not bilingualism versus English mastery. Too many children do not even master one language, a fact that is reflected in unacceptably high rates of functional illiteracy. Although this goal should be shared by every school district in the nation, we are aware that the techniques used to accomplish English mastery will need to vary from district to district. Because there is no agreement as to the most effective method for teaching English to non-English-speaking youngsters, such local variation is both necessary and desirable. **We support bilingual education as long as English mastery is the end product of the program.**

Although we believe that the development of solid basic and higher-level academic skills is the primary mission of the schools, we do not agree with some recent suggestions that schools should eliminate extracurricular activities such as athletics, music, drama, newspapers, or student government. Nor should they arbitrarily reduce instruction in physical education, music, or art in favor of exclusive concentration on academic subjects. We are convinced that this would unnecessarily penalize certain students for whom these subjects and activities form an important part of their education and an incentive for staying in school.

Indeed, we believe that these nonacademic activities not only have intrinsic value but also reinforce scholastic pursuits.* Athletics develop physical fitness, an understanding of the importance of teamwork, and a sense of competitiveness, all of which are important for achieving academic excellence and for good job performance. Music, drama, and art develop an appreciation of aesthetics and cultural awareness and require discipline and teamwork. Participation in student government or on school newspapers encourages literacy, mental discipline, and an understanding of current affairs and democratic institutions.

However, it may be desirable and necessary in some schools, where they choose, to base eligibility for participation on athletic teams or in other extracurricular pursuits on demonstrated achievement of a desired level of academic competence.

It is likely that each state's core curriculum will differ to reflect regional variations in history, literature, and other subjects. Many communities have exceptional resources, and they should be encouraged to develop them. New York City has done this with its LaGuardia High School, which combines the former Music and Art High School and the High School of the Performing Arts, and Houston with its School of Health Sciences. Some communities will have pressing problems, not shared by the nation as a whole, that will require tailored responses. For example, huge waves of immigration place greater demands for bilingual and English-language instruction in port-of-entry cities. But beneath the superficial variation lies the more important reality that any demanding academic curriculum accomplishes the same result: It instills habits of discipline, orderly thought, clear communication, and the capacity to solve problems.

In addition to identifying a core curriculum that students should master, we believe that curriculum, teaching methods and technologies, examinations, and textbooks must be integrated and coordinated and fully in tune with school board policy. They should be designed to work together, to reinforce each other, and to give the school, teacher, and student a sense of shared purpose.

EQUITY AND EXCELLENCE

Maintaining a free and open democracy demands that we actively pursue equity along with educational excellence for children who are handicapped because of race, sex, socioeconomic status, or physical dis-

---

*See memorandum by THOMAS J. EYERMAN (page 103).

ability.* Excellence and equity are not incompatible, but it will take special effort on the part of policy makers, educators, and the public to ensure that children who need more attention and resources in order to perform at acceptable levels of academic achievement are given that extra help.

One solution is to ensure access to quality education at the earliest ages through more extensive preschool training for children who are most likely to experience later educational failure. A second approach is to assure that school promotions and granting of high school diplomas are meaningful measures of achievement. Passing children through school without expecting them to demonstrate achievement helps to perpetuate the low expectations many have of the disadvantaged.

Although equity and excellence are goals of overriding national concern, implementing them on the local level often has proven to be difficult. The Houston Independent School District, for example, is dealing with these issues through a five-year strategy that stresses equity as part of its drive to achieve excellence in its schools (see below).

EQUITY AND EXCELLENCE
THE HOUSTON EXPERIENCE

The Houston Independent School District is committed to making equity a critical part of its overall strategy for achieving excellence in its public schools. Two dominant themes inspire Houston's educational philosophy: the quest for excellence in all forms of educational achievement and the need to ensure that all of the district's students have an equal opportunity to pursue excellence.

The Houston Five-Year Reform Plan has as its centerpiece a formula that describes the interrelationship between excellence and equity as a combination of factors that measure whether the goal of excellence with equity is being met. These are: financial and physical resources, validated school characteristics, and evidence of continued academic growth.

Financial and physical resources include compensation of teachers and staff, physical plant, instructional support, and transportation. Validated characteristics of effective schools include school climate, leadership, expectations, purpose, measurement of achievement, parental involvement, and quality of staffing. The Houston scheme measures the achievement of equity and excellence on the basis of predefined student outcomes, which can be demonstrated by continued academic growth. The Houston strategy places the ultimate responsibility for achieving equity and excellence squarely on the shoulders of the individual school, its teachers, and, especially, its principal.

*See memorandum by DONALD E. GUINN (page 102).

STANDARDS AND PERFORMANCE MEASURES

Customarily, school promotion and the awarding of high school diplomas are determined by the number of years a student has attended school, presumably with passing grades. But we are convinced that promotion without demonstrated achievement is a mistake that benefits no one, certainly not the student. Too often, the policies of social promotion and easy graduation result in a young adult who, bereft of meaningful literacy and other job skills, becomes just another statistic on the unemployment charts and welfare rolls.

Alongside efforts to raise standards for all students, we strongly urge that increased efforts be made to raise the performance of lower-achieving students in order to reduce the unacceptably high percentage of those students who are dropping out of the nation's schools. Higher standards for all must accompany greater efforts for the minority that have the greatest difficulty performing at adequate levels of academic achievement.

MAKING DIPLOMAS MEANINGFUL

The high school diploma should indicate that a student has met or exceeded an established standard of achievement, and we urge all states to establish a minimum standard of performance for awarding a diploma.

But minimum standards are not enough. If students demonstrate above average or outstanding achievement, they should be rewarded. **We endorse the concept of awarding honors diplomas to signify superior accomplishment.** We believe that such a practice would provide an incentive for students to work harder because their diplomas would have increased meaning for employers and society. Several approaches are worth considering. For years, New York State has awarded Regents diplomas to students who have taken and passed statewide achievement examinations in specific subject areas. Diplomas could be awarded at varying levels of distinction, following the lead of colleges and universities and most European nations. A third alternative would be a general diploma accompanied by a statement of accomplishment in particular subject areas.

DEVELOPING EFFECTIVE PERFORMANCE MEASURES

For such a system to work, schools must begin to set performance standards for all their students and to develop the necessary measuring tools to gauge whether they have learned the skills and knowledge that are supposed to be taught. With such effective measures at their disposal, local schools could allocate their time appropriately in order to meet state standards.

In the past two years, almost every state in the nation has legislated regular achievement testing at specific intervals. Most of these statewide efforts focus on the acquisition of basic skills in reading, writing, and mathematics in those grades designated as "promotional gates." Generally, this means that youngsters will have to demonstrate adequate development of basic skills in the third, fifth, or eighth grades (the actual grade level at which such testing is required varies from state to state) and will not be promoted to the next grade until their performance is up to par.

We applaud the trend toward periodic testing to evaluate whether basic skills have been acquired, and we recommend that all states and localities which have not already done so should immediately adopt this practice. However, in the rush to evaluate basic skills, school officials should guard against the tendency to test acquisition of minimum skills only. Rather than provide a satisfactory diagnostic tool, minimum skills testing would only burden the schools with unproductive testing instruments. Tests should be designed so that they measure fairly and equitably what children at specific stages of development should be expected to do and know, such as read for content and comprehension, learn effectively, make judgments and deductions, write coherently, and apply critical thinking skills to solving problems, both in language and in mathematics.

We believe that as students mature they should be expected to demonstrate greater retention of course content and information in addition to grade-level reading, writing, and mathematics skills. Beginning with the middle grades, achievement tests that measure specific course content should begin to be phased into the testing program. Without content, the problem-solving skills we know are necessary for success in a highly complex world would be nearly impossible to develop.

In addition, we believe that mastery of basic skills and subject content should not be judged solely by the ability to pass multiple-choice, true-or-false, or machine-scored examinations. Proper testing of written expression and comprehension is crucial for evaluation of mastery in the early grades, when the foundations for all subsequent learning are established.

We also believe that the purpose of testing is primarily evaluative and diagnostic. The results of standardized examinations in reading, mathematics, verbal expression and comprehension, or reasoning skills should be used to measure student achievement. Such tests should be diagnostic for such purposes as redesigning ineffective curricula or teaching methods or for assigning remedial work to students who need it. Testing also has a long-range purpose. Appropriate tests provide a measure of how the school system is doing and how student achievement levels are changing over time.

Proper and adequate testing is the only sure way we have of finding out whether our schoolchildren are learning. Without effective evaluation procedures, there is no way for our schools to identify their weak points or develop an adequate basis on which to promulgate improvement strategies. Without testing there is no way to help the child who is falling behind before his or her deficiencies become too widespread or too ingrained to be remedied.

PARENTAL RESPONSIBILITY

We cannot overemphasize the important role of parents in helping their children to attain educational excellence. More parents should take an active interest in their children's homework and in school programs in general. Parents should view the results of diagnostic and achievement tests, not only as a school responsibility, but as an indication of their need to participate in helping their children improve in school.

Business has two important roles that it can perform to help parents become more involved in their children's schooling and more responsible for their academic achievement. **First, we recommend that businesses make a special effort to support the involvement of all their employees who are parents in their children's schooling and to provide information about schools and education issues to all interested employees.** Employee networks can be encouraged to provide parents with ways of communicating with one another.

Second, we recommend that business develop flexible policies which allow and encourage both parents and interested nonparents, especially those who are hourly employees, to participate actively in their community's schools. This is particularly important because of the growing numbers of single-parent and two-career families.

THE SCHOOL/BUSINESS INTERCHANGE

Identifying the mutual needs of business and students can help schools develop an integrated and relevant curriculum that reflects the realities of the job market. A rapidly changing work environment emphasizes the need for continuous communication between schools and the business community. **We recommend the development of a feedback mechanism through**

which employers can keep the schools informed about the performance of their graduates in the workplace.

As part of its mission to provide information on how the nation's students are doing, the NAEP should make a regular assessment of the job readiness of the nation's high school graduates. (For a more detailed discussion, see Chapter 3, page 50.)

Schools also need to provide better links between education and the world of work. In Chapter 5, we cite numerous examples of business/school partnerships that focus on the school-to-work transition. School guidance counselors should be able to help students make informed choices regarding job paths, but as presently performed, the counseling function is usually a weak link between school and work. **We recommend that school systems assign a high priority to upgrading the counseling function of their guidance departments, particularly at the junior high or middle school level, where many students begin to make important decisions about their futures.**

MONY FINANCIAL SERVICES
ADOPT-A-KID

In 1984, the MONY Financial Services Company, located in Purchase, New York, initiated an innovative partnership, called "Adopt-a-Kid," with the schools in nearby Port Chester. Located in affluent Westchester County, Port Chester, unlike most of its neighboring communities, has a large poor, minority, and disadvantaged population. The aim of the MONY-Port Chester program is to provide severely disadvantaged children with successful adult role models.

In its first year, the program paired twenty MONY employees with an equal number of children at the Kennedy Elementary School. Initial lunchtime visits to the school and the workplace were arranged by the company. After these introductory sessions, the volunteers were expected to continue the relationship in a way that best suited them and the child. Some of the volunteers developed traditional "big brother" or "sister" relationships, by taking the child on trips to the movies, going shopping, or participating in other joint activities. Others developed a regular written correspondence with their child. The program has been so successful that the company plans to expand it to eighty students and volunteers in its second year.

MONY also recognizes the need for successful adult role models for disadvantaged teenagers, and it is in the process of developing a similar partnership with the Port Chester high school. This program will involve employees in small group sessions that are designed to broaden the students' knowledge of adult roles and career possibilities.

Business can contribute to providing improved guidance. **We recommend that local business leaders contribute to the efforts of school counselors by providing some appropriate form of sponsorship for those students who are likely to have the greatest difficulty entering the job market, especially low achievers from poor families. These students tend to have few role models on which to pattern their own workplace efforts.** One company that is trying to address the need for disadvantaged youngsters to have successful adult role models outside of their families is MONY Financial Services, which has initiated a partnership program called "Adopt-a-Kid" (see page 27).

LESSONS FROM BUSINESS MANAGEMENT: A MARKET APPROACH

Accountability and responsiveness in public education cannot be legislated, regulated, or achieved by fiat or good intentions alone. They require both incentives and disincentives. The system that best meets these objectives fairly, efficiently, and rapidly is a market system.

Most students are assigned to schools by accident of geography and are required by law to attend schools in their immediate neighborhoods. It is no wonder that schools, lacking competition, exhibit many of the characteristics of monopolies. As a public-sector activity, schools will never be subject to the full play of the market. Nevertheless, we believe that certain market incentives and disincentives can and should be introduced into public schooling. For example, regional or even statewide open-enrollment systems would make it possible for children and their families to choose from among a wide variety of public schools. Such freedom of choice would reward schools that met the educational objectives of the families that select them and send a message to those schools that are bypassed.

One outcome would be product differentiation: Schools could tailor their offerings to their clients in the same way businesses must if they want to survive in a competitive environment. Magnet schools, which draw students from outside the neighborhood by offering special programs, are an example of such differentiation. We believe the evidence in favor of magnet schools is strong enough to warrant widespread support for increasing their number. Taking this a step further, a state or region might adopt a "universal" magnet school plan, in which every school in the jurisdiction is open to every student in the area. Unlike voucher or tax credit proposals that include private schools, the universal magnet school would not put the public school system at risk. Instead, it would give individual public schools the opportunity to succeed or fail by introducing market mechanisms into the public sector.

IMPROVING SCHOOL MANAGEMENT

The business community can offer some important insights into some of the problems of educational management and organization. Two strategies used by business, bankruptcy and affording exceptional units special treatment, may have valuable application as tools for measuring and acting on the performance of the educational organization. Schools and school districts can and should be expected to reach clearly enunciated goals and objectives, but if they do not, the state or local school authorities should have the power to take effective action.

Educational Bankruptcy. Bankruptcy can be applied to school organizations in the same way that it is used in business. When a school district grossly fails to meet its obligations to its students, it should be placed in "receivership;" it should then be reorganized, or arrangements should be made to transfer its assets and liabilities. The state or local educational authority invoking receivership would be responsible for seeing that the delinquent school is brought up to standard, goals are clearly and realistically designed and articulated, management improved, and resources allocated effectively.

Special Schools, Special Treatment. Many successful corporations exempt special units from following strict company procedures as a way of encouraging innovation. So far as we know, there has been no systematic attempt at the state level to apply this strategy to the public schools. In part this is understandable. Waiving the rules for one school or one district would represent a departure in government practice. We believe, however, that it is time to consider making such a departure. **Borrowing from business practice, we recommend that states, by rule or law, exempt their best performing school districts from prescriptive statutes, rules, and regulations so that those districts can be free to design programs through which they can best accomplish their educational objectives.** We do not believe that officials in state capitals know as much about effective schools as the teachers and administrators in their best school districts do.

The North Carolina School of Science and Mathematics provides a good example of how relaxation of prescriptive state rules can have a positive effect on organization and management. Although it is subject to general state standards, it has an independent board of trustees, may select its own textbooks, and may hire uncertified teachers. Rather than encouraging the selection of inappropriate textbooks and lower-cost teachers, just the opposite has occurred. We are convinced that other high-quality schools across the nation would behave in the same way if they were free to do so.

VOCATIONAL EDUCATION

If there is any aspect of secondary schooling in which employability is an appropriate measure of quality, it is vocational education. We define the chief purpose of vocational education as preparing students for future jobs. Unfortunately, whether measured by future earnings, job placement, or employment success, there is today little evidence that vocational education is either meeting the needs of students or of the employers who are expected to hire them. Moreover, vocational education too often perpetuates sex role stereotyping and tracking of minorities into inferior programs.

Overall, vocational education can be credited with preparing but a small fraction of students for future work. Only in the areas of business and office skills and agricultural skills does there appear to be a direct link between the vocational instruction students receive in school and their future careers.

Some educators argue that vocational education has a number of purposes beyond imparting employability skills. These include instruction in life skills, such as those taught in home economics or shop, and job exploration. Perhaps more important, vocational education claims to serve as a device to encourage youths who are not succeeding academically to stay in school. If this view has validity, then it is most important to ensure that staying in school also means developing basic academic skills that will pay off for these students in the future.

REDEFINING VOCATIONAL EDUCATION

Measured by current definitions, as many as 95 percent of all secondary school students take some form of vocational education, and 80 percent participate in some form of occupationally specific instruction. All education is "vocational" in that one of its purposes is to prepare young people to be employable. If the term "vocational education" is to have any useful meaning, it must be more narrowly defined. **We believe that the term *vocational education* should be limited to those programs that are specifically designed to prepare students to enter a field upon graduation. All other forms of nonacademic instruction should be identified by a different term to avoid confusing them with curricula designed to impart specific job skills.**

In addition, all of these programs need to be judged by standards that evaluate their contribution to the employability of high school graduates.

Accordingly, we would suggest that distinctions be made among the following:

1. Programs geared toward specific entry-level positions.

2. Exploratory programs to assist in career choice.

3. Job search and general employability skills, such as how to behave in an interview and getting to work on time.

4. Employment counseling.

5. Enrollments in joint ventures with employers such as cooperative education.

However it is defined, vocational education requires substantial improvement. In our analysis of vocational education we conclude that there are two fundamental reasons why vocational education so often appears to be ineffective for preparing secondary students for the job market. First, too many students in occupationally specific vocational education programs have simply not had the necessary grounding in basic academic and behavioral skills that are the minimum required for most entry-level positions in today's labor market. Second, vocational education students too often learn nonacademic or vocational skills that do not relate to the kinds of jobs that are normally available in the economy.

ACADEMICS FIRST

For many vocational education students, a history of poor academic achievement develops long before they make the choice to select an occupationally specific program. Remedying this will require much greater attention to the basics while children are in elementary and junior high school. **We believe better and earlier academic instruction will ensure that if a student chooses to take occupationally specific training, that student will not only perform better in the classroom, but also will have the fundamental communication, computational, and problem-solving skills that are required by virtually all of today's employers for entry-level positions.**

Students who are poorly prepared academically by the time they reach high school frequently need substantial remedial work, which too often is provided by vocational instructors who are ill-equipped for that demanding task. One result is that vocational instructors spend proportionally less time delivering quality job-specific training.

Therefore, we recommend the following strategy to improve the achievement of vocational education students: Before any student is

allowed to complete occupationally specific training, he or she should be required to demonstrate achievement of an adequate level of academic competence. Similarly, vocational education majors should be expected to complete a core academic curriculum in addition to occupationally specific training.

We also recognize that academic standards developed to assess minimum academic competency may need to be adjusted for certain types of students, such as the mentally retarded and learning disabled. For the general population of students, the neglect of academic standards has limited their long-term employment opportunities. Basics do not compete with vocational skills; they help lay the foundations for all types of learning. Vocational instruction at the expense of quality instruction in the basics is a disservice to the students who participate in these programs.

Individual programs have been successful in integrating the basics with occupational training, but these usually involve high-quality instructors who see this as a major objective of the program. Unfortunately, this is not a widespread practice.

MEETING LABOR MARKET NEEDS

However it is viewed, vocational education, with few exceptions, has failed to make a measurable impact on the success of its graduates in the labor market because too much of what is offered in vocational programs does not relate to the available jobs. A recent report by the U.S. Labor Department's Bureau of Labor Statistics supports this contention.[4] It found that high school level occupationally specific programs accounted for only 5 percent of all the sources of training for those jobs that need specific occupational training.

One exception to the poor track record of occupationally specific programs is secretarial training. Of all the nation's secretaries, 35 percent received their training in high school vocational programs in business and office skills. Yet outside of this area and certain drafting, agricultural, auto mechanics, and crafts programs, there appear to be few vocational programs that justify the investment in them.

The same holds true for courses that are not job specific, yet are called vocational education. It is unclear how useful these courses are as an investment of student time. While traditional shop and introductory home economics courses may impart worthwhile life skills, beyond a period of time these courses rapidly hit a point of diminishing returns.

Exploratory programs also appear to be of minimal value as vocational education. Industrial arts, perhaps the most common exploratory program,

---

4. Bureau of Labor Statistics, U.S. Department of Labor, *Occupational Outlook Quarterly* (Winter 1984), pp. 2-21.

often involves little more than woodworking, and only rarely the other industrial arts, such as metal fabrication. Although these courses provide valuable hands-on experience and exposure that students might not otherwise get, they do not provide an accurate sense of the modern workplace and should not be offered as job exploration or in lieu of basic academic courses.

JOINT PROGRAMS WITH EMPLOYERS

Despite these negative findings, there are certain types of vocational programs that can make an important contribution to a student's later employability. One example is cooperative education, which is a carefully worked out joint program between schools and employers. Cooperative education students spend two to three hours a day in an occupationally specific vocational class and two to three hours in a carefully selected job outside of the school, usually in the private sector. Cooperative education has grown in popularity, expanding tenfold in the past decade. Today, three-quarters of a million students participate. The Murry Bergtraum School for Banking and Finance Careers, described in Chapter 5 on page 93, is an example of a particularly successful cooperative program.

Although there have been few formal assessments of cooperative education, the available research suggests that it results in better performance by students both in school and after graduation. The key to the program's success is that it stresses academic instruction as an integrated part of the vocational curriculum. This and other career-based work experience programs appear to improve a student's future labor market success and earnings potential. **On the basis of its record, we encourage a careful expansion of cooperative education and similar programs, particularly in schools where they do not now exist, combined with a more thorough analysis of the program's outcome. We also recommend that business participate in such efforts.**

IMPROVING THE QUALITY OF INSTRUCTION

Another major reason for the poor overall performance of vocational education is the extreme unevenness in quality from state to state, locality to locality, and school to school. Programs range from the highly regarded technical schools, such as Baltimore Polytechnic and Aviation High School in New York City, which are highly competitive, to generalized vocational schools that tend to combine the worst of both the vocational and the general academic programs.

In general, area vocational schools, which centralize technical equipment and other support services in a more cost-effective manner, appear to provide better-quality instruction and a greater range of vocational resources. On the other hand, vocational high schools that offer a general range of vocational subjects (as opposed to the occupationally specific programs of such schools as Aviation High School) and most neighborhood comprehensive high schools are usually inferior. The reason these schools fail to prepare their students adequately for the job market is clear: Both vocational schools and comprehensive high schools generally offer their vocational students inferior academic programs.

In school districts with area vocational centers, the general high school is devoted almost exclusively to academic preparation, and the result is that the best of both the vocational and the academic curricula are brought to bear. **Therefore, we recommend that more attention be paid to developing area vocational centers and to the gradual elimination of separate and unequal comprehensive and vocational high schools.**

We recognize the difficulty of implementing this approach throughout the country. Indeed, in some areas this approach may be impractical, particularly in rural school systems where transportation is a problem and where there may be only one area high school to begin with. But overall we believe that the area center has shown itself to be a superior form for delivering vocational instruction.

Another possible approach to improving access to and delivery of vocational programs involves contracting for vocational education services to bring the expertise of proprietary vocational schools into the public schools. Such contracting to private suppliers for instructional services may be workable in areas where the public schools lack sufficient resources to develop their own high-quality programs. **Therefore, we recommend limited trial programs to test the use of contracting to private suppliers for vocational education services in the public schools, where appropriate.**

THE ROLE OF BUSINESS

Business has an important stake in improving vocational education. In fact, it was the business community that convinced the federal government to pass the original vocational education statute of 1917. Recent major surveys by the National Association of Manufacturers and the United States Chamber of Commerce indicate that this support continues.

Yet, we believe that few business people have a clear sense of what vocational education is and how it is being delivered in the nation's schools. Few recognize that vocational education has grown to encompass a variety of purposes, most of which have nothing to do with preparing a student for the world of work. One reason is that there are no adequate means to measure whether vocational education is succeeding. In our view, such measuring tools need to include as a basis for judgment both competency in basic skills and future earnings and employment potential.

The business community needs to take the lead in sorting out what vocational education is and what it ought to do. Business should help design the measurements by which vocational education is to be judged. Finally, the business community needs to see that vocational education is well-equipped, delivers quality instruction, and graduates employable students. Unless these things are done, the greatest losers will be the students themselves.

The Carl D. Perkins Vocational Education Act of 1984 offers the business community a unique opportunity to accomplish these goals at the federal, state, and local levels. First, private industry will represent a majority on the National Council on Vocational Education. This will not only help bring business into a more active dialogue on vocational issues at the national level, but will help focus on the need to assure that vocational education is responsive to the changing needs of labor markets. Second, the State Councils on Vocational Education are now required to have majority representation by employers and union leaders. This will help monitor the effectiveness of the delivery of existing programs. Third, the new law establishes Technical Committees, comprised almost entirely of employers, to advise state boards of education on various aspects of vocational education. Of special importance is the role of these committees, who, in partnership with educators, will advise the state boards on needed curriculum changes and help to define priority occupational areas within a state.

We believe that the new federal vocational statute offers business an opportunity to have a positive impact on vocational education and to improve the quality of vocational graduates. **We encourage corporations to participate in the newly redesigned advisory and technical committees as established under the Carl D. Perkins Vocational Education Act of 1984.**

In conclusion, vocational education needs new focus and substantial improvement if it is to remain a viable part of secondary schooling. This will depend in large measure on improving the academic competence of vocational students and on ensuring that vocational offerings are relevant to the needs of the labor market.

CHAPTER 3

INVESTMENT STRATEGIES IN EDUCATION

A sound public education system is the most important investment this nation can make in its future. The right investment decisions can yield handsome returns both for the individual and for the economy; the wrong ones may jeopardize efforts to redesign an education system that is productive for all children.

The success of education reform will depend not only on *how much* we invest in education, but also on *how wisely* we invest our available resources. Although standards need to be set and guidance provided by state and local education authorities, it is in each individual school and each classroom that improvements in learning will occur. It will take commitment and effort by state and local leaders, principals, teachers, and parents to assure that the resources available to the schools are invested where they will result in the highest possible learning gains for students.

Many of the specific reforms we advocate in this report will require increasing our present level of investment in education. Although resources at all levels of government are being constrained, we believe that the nation is underinvesting in public education. A larger investment is essential and has the potential for a very significant return in both human and financial terms. **With its strong stake in quality education, the business community should give increased investment in public education its wholehearted support.**

Although we support increased spending on public education, we believe that increases should go only to well-designed reforms that are coupled with clearly defined goals and effective strategies for achieving specific objectives. It is imperative that strategies for investment in education reflect a concern for cost-effectiveness and demonstrate an understanding of the principles of effective resource management. Cutting waste and inefficiency are necessary adjuncts to increased funding for the schools.

In this chapter we identify investments in education that are likely to produce a very high return for the nation. The evidence points to the clear need to increase our investment in:

- **Preschool Programs for the Disadvantaged.** Enriched, early education for children at risk substantially increases the likelihood of success in later schooling and bolsters economic and social performance.

- **Elementary Education.** For the majority of children, the foundations for all subsequent learning are laid in the early grades. This is where the most intense efforts should be focused to develop the broad range of communication, learning, and behavioral skills that are vital to later success in school and work.

- **Junior High School.** Junior high and middle schools have generally been neglected as targets of reform, yet most experts agree that this is where some of the most serious educational problems can be found. At the junior high school level, young adolescents reach a critical turning point in their education. For low achievers, junior high is where poor attitudes and performance become firmly established, and where potential dropouts can usually be identified. For all youngsters, junior high is pivotal in developing problem-solving skills as well as an interest in science and mathematics.

- **Helping Dropouts.** For those whom the school system has failed, the Job Corps, which combines work experience with remedial education in a residential setting, has been shown to be a successful model for compensatory education.

- **Research and Data Collection.** Over the long term, the principal source of increased educational quality will stem from the application of high-quality research. Particularly important will be data collected at the federal level that allows comparisons to be made in educational performance locally, statewide, and nationally.

This chapter is divided into two sections. The first examines the importance of education as an investment for individuals and society and where the most cost-effective investments in education are likely to be. The second deals with how education is financed and who is responsible for decisions on allocation of resources.

THE ECONOMICS OF EDUCATION[1]

Education is a costly activity not only because it requires paying for teachers, books, buildings, and other resources, but also because it requires time that could be used for other valuable activities. However, education produces both monetary and noneconomic benefits to the individual who is being educated, to his or her family, and to society in general.

From an economic standpoint, the major benefit of education to the individual is the higher compensation that can be expected to result from a higher level of educational attainment. There are four probable reasons for this.

■ First, higher earnings are identified with the greater skill and productivity of a more educated worker. Similarly, subsequent training is more likely to be offered to those who already have skills.

■ Second, those with more education are expected to be more adept at making good decisions and at using resources in the most effective ways; they are expected to be able to use their skills, machinery, and other resources more efficiently.

■ Third, schools teach students behavior and attitudes appropriate to the work ethic of their society, thereby contributing to a more efficient and productive work environment.

■ Fourth, schools are institutions that sort students according to different productive traits. Higher levels of schooling are therefore a signal to prospective employers that the person is likely to be more productive.

---

1. The sections on the economics of education and on investments in education are based in large part on Daniel H. Saks, "A Legacy for the 21st Century: Investment Opportunities in Our Children's Schooling," an unpublished paper prepared for the Committee for Economic Development's Subcommittee on Business and the Schools, 1984.

EVALUATING RETURNS ON
OUR INVESTMENT IN EDUCATION

Business people are used to evaluating investments in terms of their rates of return, while weighing relative costs and benefits. In evaluating the rates of return on investments in schooling, economists have traditionally focused on the returns received from each additional year of education. Unfortunately, there is almost no reliable analysis of the returns that can be expected from differences in the quality of education for any given number of years of education completed.

Consequently, we recommend that a serious effort be made by the National Assessment of Educational Progress (NAEP) or some other reliable body to establish a regular analysis of benefits received from improving the content and quality of education in addition to currently available analyses of benefits derived from increased years of education.

The best current estimate of average rates of return on our investment in schooling range from 7 to 11 percent after inflation, which makes education a very good personal and societal investment. Even when the costs incurred by society in providing education are excluded, schooling returns more to the economy than it takes out. This is even truer when one considers that higher levels of education also lower the likelihood of unemployment and generate higher salaries and fringe benefits.

There are also many noneconomic benefits that can accrue to individuals from more and better education. For example, more highly educated people tend to be both more knowledgeable and more willing to invest in better health for themselves, which shows up in lower mortality rates. They also tend to be more efficient consumers and to raise healthier children who perform better in school. More highly educated people also tend to save more and to plan better for the future. Such behavior is an important component of social growth and welfare.

Other benefits accrue to society as well. Violent crime is reduced by an increase in education. In addition, more education presumably produces more knowledgeable citizens who are better able to make important decisions, weigh issues, and make reasonably well-informed political choices.

QUALITY, NOT QUANTITY

At the turn of the century only 6.4 percent of seventeen-year-olds in this country were high school graduates. Today, about three-quarters of all eighteen-year-olds have graduated from high school. Throughout this century, and especially since World War II, education has been an important component of the growth in the U.S. economy. However, the main source of this growth has been an increase in the average number of years of schooling rather than improvements in the quality of each year of education.

Now that a majority of the work force has graduated from high school, it is likely that returns from this investment will diminish as the opportunities for growth in output per worker decrease. The same may be true of trying to increase the proportion of the population who have obtained a college degree. However, we believe that there are substantial opportunities for yielding very high returns from improvements in quality, rather than from increasing the number of years of education completed.

THE COSTS OF FAILURE

Although very difficult to quantify, it is evident that failing to make a necessary and sufficient investment to improve education can have serious consequences for individuals and for society. If we examine the high rates of functional illiteracy among adults in this nation as just one benchmark of educational failure, the costs in terms of lost productivity and wages and increased welfare and crime are staggering. Adult illiteracy is costly to individuals who are unemployable or who cannot work productively and to the businesses that may employ them. Moreover, adults who cannot read cannot help their children in school.

Based on 1980 census data, the U.S. Department of Education estimates that 23 million adults over the age of eighteen are functionally illiterate and incapable of performing on the job in any but the most menial tasks. An additional 46 million adults are considered to be just marginally literate.

Broken down by race and socioeconomic status, these figures are even more alarming, and have important implications for education policy in urban areas. According to the 1980 census data, as many as 44 percent of blacks and 56 percent of Hispanics over the age of eighteen are functionally illiterate, as are 40 percent of all adults earning less than $5,000 a year. One-third of mothers who receive welfare benefits are illiterate, and approximately three-quarters of the prison population have never completed high school. In addition, the army has reported that as many as 27 percent of army enlistees cannot read training manuals written at the seventh-grade level.[2]

This high level of academic failure has many possible consequences. From an economic standpoint, it means that a sizable part of our labor pool will be made up of people with marginal skills who are poorly matched to the job market. The result would be chronically higher rates of unemployment, higher welfare costs, less personal income, and a smaller tax base. Increasingly high rates of functional and marginal illiteracy are also likely to lead to rising crime rates, a lower standard of living, and social instability.

2. B. Dalton Bookseller, "National Literacy Initiative," 1985.

Finally, a large portion of the nation's population would lack important decision-making skills, which could have serious implications for the future of the United States as a free and democratic republic.

At least two major corporations, B. Dalton Bookseller and Time Inc., are attempting to reverse these high illiteracy rates (see below).

CHOOSING WISE INVESTMENTS

If we want to get the best return on our education dollar, we will have to analyze very carefully and systematically where our best educational investments lie. Among the factors that will affect future investments are the new demographic forces that are radically changing the makeup of our population. These demographic shifts offer planners both opportunities and challenges, generating the need for well-thought-out changes in school programs and policies. The figures on pages 42 and 43 illustrate some of the

CONQUERING ILLITERACY
B. DALTON BOOKSELLER AND TIME INC.

B. Dalton Bookseller, headquartered in Minneapolis, has spearheaded a national drive to recruit volunteers to tutor illiterate adults individually through a variety of community-based organizations. The company provides funding, management, and employee support for programs implemented by public and nonprofit organizations that possess the necessary expertise and knowledge to make an impact on the illiteracy problem.

Part of B. Dalton's rationale for focusing on adult illiterates is its belief that illiterate parents are unprepared or unable to provide the kind of parental support and involvement needed to help their children do well in school. B. Dalton's primary goal is to provide by 1986 individual tutoring for 100,000 illiterate adults each year. To accomplish this, the company is providing funding to 300 local programs around the country to help train 50,000 volunteer tutors each year.

Time Inc. has launched a pilot program, called "Time to Read," which is designed to reach both schoolchildren who need remedial help and adult illiterates as well. This program utilizes employee volunteers and Time Inc. publications in person-to-person tutoring at Time Inc. locations. Four pilot programs have been launched in 1985 in New York; Chicago; Charlotte, North Carolina; and Kansas City, Missouri. "Time to Read" works with community organizations in those cities to recruit students and provide support services.

changes in family composition and income levels affecting school-age children.

■ **The school population.** A new baby boom is projected to increase public school enrollment in the United States through the rest of this century. However, an increasing proportion of these students will be black and Hispanic and will live in single-parent homes. By the year 2000, minorities will make up the majority of the school-age population in fifty-three major American cities.

■ **The adult population.** The population is getting older, and, for the first time in this nation's history, those now over sixty-five outnumber teenagers. This may cause severe competition for resources targeted for social programs versus education.

■ **The teacher work force.** Since 1979, the U.S. teacher population has steadily declined. The combination of a shrinking teacher population and a growing student population will present significant opportunities for young and able college graduates to enter the profession.

THE CHANGING DEMOGRAPHICS OF SCHOOL-AGE CHILDREN

In 1983, three out of every five black children lived in single-parent homes, most of which were headed by women.

Percent of Persons Under 18 Years Old Living With Both Parents, 1970 and 1983

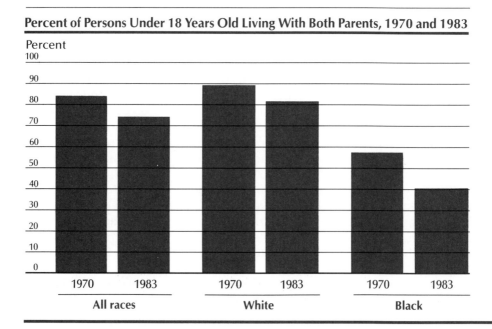

Planning for wise educational investments must take into account the fact that quality education is a developmental process; successful completion of each level of schooling provides the intellectual foundation for the level that follows. **We are convinced that the earliest stages of educational development, elementary school and preschool for disadvantaged children, are where we will receive the best return on our educational investment. Moreover, we consider the junior high or middle school to be at least as important as a focus of education reform.**

PRESCHOOL PROGRAMS

Preschool programs that provide developmental training for three- or four-year-olds have generated a great deal of controversy over the past two decades. Despite early findings to the contrary, well-designed studies now make it clear that high-quality preschool programs lasting one year and targeted to four-year-olds from poor families can have enormous economic payoffs.

And children from such homes were most likely to be living in poverty. Almost 60 percent of children in female-headed, single-parent homes had families with incomes under $10,000. Some 46 percent of all black children and 38 percent of all Hispanic children lived in poverty, compared to 22 percent for children of all races.

Children in Families, by Total 1982 Family Income and Family Type, 1983

Percent of Own Children 17 Years and Under in Families, 1983

1982 Income	All Families	Married-Couple Families	Families Maintained by Women, No Husband Present
Under $5,000	8.0%	3.1%	29.6%
$5,000-9,999	10.8	6.5	29.4
10,000-14,999	11.7	10.5	16.8
15,000-19,999	11.5	11.8	10.1
20,000-24,999	12.4	13.7	6.9
25,000 and over	45.5	54.5	7.2
Total	100.0	100.0	100.0

SOURCE: *DataTrack 14, Children* (Washington, D.C.: American Council of Life Insurance, December 1984), pp. 13 and 21.

Preschool programs illustrate three critical points about the economics of schooling: First, it is important to target on high-risk groups. Second, the developmental view of schooling is crucial; small differences in performance in the early years of schooling accumulate over a student's early life to produce dramatic differences in performance as young adults. Third, well-designed long-term research is essential to the reliable identification of cumulative program benefits occurring years after program completion.

In examining the effectiveness of preschool education, a study of the Perry Preschool Program in Ypsilanti, Michigan, described in greater detail on opposite page, stands as a model of education research.[3]

If we examine the Perry Preschool Program for its investment return and convert all costs and benefits into current values based on a 3 percent real rate of interest, one year of the program is an extraordinary economic buy. It would be hard to imagine that society could find a higher yield for a dollar of investment than that found in preschool programs for its at-risk children. Of course, such judgments depend on whether the differences in employment and college attendance rates will persist past age nineteen as the project researchers predict they will. But even if their estimates are off by several hundred percent, the return would be exceedingly high relative to other investment opportunities.

What contributed to the effectiveness of the Perry Preschool Program? To begin with, those who went through the program tended to be treated somewhat differently by teachers later in their school careers. Although many of those in the control group were regarded as mentally retarded and were shunted into expensive special education classes during their regular school years, the students from the preschool program were viewed as simply needing extra help, which seems to have been provided in many cases. Both teachers and students behaved as if learning problems could be addressed successfully in the context of the regular classroom.

Even more important, researchers attribute success to high-quality program design and operation, including curriculum implementation, parental involvement, staff supervision, in-service training, teacher planning, staff relationships, on-going evaluation, and administrative leadership. These are the same elements that have been identified as characteristics of effective schools in general.

Another follow-up study of participants in a much larger Head Start program in Harlem in New York City has yielded results similar to the Ypsilanti study. This study, conducted by researchers at the New York University School of Education, examined the progress of 178 young people, aged nineteen-to-twenty-one, who had participated in an extensive Head Start

3. John R. B. Clements, Lawrence J. Schwinhart, W. Steven Barnett, Ann S. Epstein, and David P. Weikart, *Changed Lives: The Effects of the Perry Preschool Program on Youths Through Age Nineteen* (Ypsilanti, Michigan: The High-Scope Press, 1984).

program in the mid-1960s. The researchers found that those who participated in the early education program had an employment rate double that of a control group, were 50 percent more likely to have graduated from high school, and were about one-third more likely to have gone on to some form of postsecondary education.

By 1980, some 37 percent of all three- and four-year-olds in this country were enrolled in early childhood education programs, excluding custodial day care. However, only 19 percent of three-year-olds from families with incomes under $10,000 and only 29 percent of four-year-olds from such families were enrolled in early childhood education programs in 1980.

Although preschool education programs may be beneficial for most four-year-olds, they are clearly desirable for four-year-olds from disadvan-

---

THE PERRY PRESCHOOL PROGRAM

Approximately 100 children eligible for preschool programs between 1962 and 1967 took part in the Perry Preschool Program in Ypsilanti, Michigan. All were from extremely poor minority families and each was judged to have a low intelligence quotient. Almost half the children lived in single-parent homes, and fewer than 20 percent of the parents had completed high school. Half of the children were randomly assigned to the preschool program; the other half, also randomly chosen, did not participate in any kind of preschool program. The students in both groups have been closely monitored for over fifteen years. This means that any differences between the two groups can reliably be attributed to the effects of the program.

The program was directed at the intellectual and social development of the participating three- and four-year-olds. For one school year, from October to May, the students were in class for two and a half hours each morning, Monday through Friday. There was one adult teacher for every five or six children, and teachers made home visits to each mother and child for approximately one and a half hours each week. Those who administered the tests, interviews, and follow-up studies over the years did not know which children had been in the preschool program. Their analysis revealed significant differences in the achievement of both academic and social skills at age nineteen between those who did and those who did not participate in the preschool program fifteen years earlier. Employment and college or vocational training rates for the preschool group are almost double; the high school graduation rate is almost one-third higher; arrest rates are 40 percent lower; and teenage pregnancy rates are almost half. Furthermore, on a test of functional competence those who went through the preschool program were more than 50 percent more likely to score at or above the national average and to have spent only half as many years in special education programs as those who did not.

taged families. It appears to be the margin of difference that can have substantial effects on the later economic and social performance of these children. Enriched, early education for at-risk children substantially increases their likelihood of success in grade school, junior high, and high school. It also reduces juvenile delinquency and crime, and adult dependency is reduced through decreased rates of incarceration, joblessness, and welfare.

We believe that local school districts, with the encouragement and support of their state governments, should undertake a serious and systematic investment in enriched early childhood education for children from poor families. Such programs should be available to all four-year-olds from impoverished backgrounds in every school district for one year before they enter kindergarten. Funding a new program of this kind is not simply a matter of resource reallocation. If one program must be traded for another, early childhood education for high-risk children should exert a very strong claim on state and local budgets.

We do not expect optimum results from these programs in their first years of operation, but we do believe that the possibility of future returns far outweighs the pitfalls. We also recognize that we will have to continue to learn more about effective preschool programs in order to adjust existing programs. Because this issue is of national scope and interest, preschool education is a subject ideally suited to research and study by the federal government.

PRIMARY SCHOOL PERFORMANCE

Primary schooling appears to be one of the stronger elements of the American education system. But even though the average performance at the primary level is satisfactory, there are great variations and many opportunities for improvement.

At the elementary level, major federal investment in compensatory programs seems to have made a positive impact on achievement. The test scores of third and fourth graders have shown dramatic improvement in the past decade, especially in basic reading. The increases were most pronounced for those who had the worst risk of fourth-grade reading deficiencies: blacks, children from rural and disadvantaged urban communities, and those living in the southeastern United States. Undoubtedly, this reflects the increased emphasis throughout the country on teaching of reading as the primary mission of elementary schools.

Unfortunately, these gains seem to dissipate during the junior high school years, although for the most at-risk students, the elementary schools have been building a better foundation in basic reading skills. It is also worth noting that as efforts were directed more toward reading, scores in science achievement began to decline — a reminder that schools are productive enterprises and if they produce more of one thing, they may produce less of something else. **A double-sided response is called for: First, research is needed to determine how the progress made in reading achievement in the early grades can be sustained through the junior high school years. Second, the schools must find ways to teach simultaneously reading and other important subjects, such as science and mathematics.**

THE TRANSITION YEARS:
FOCUS ON JUNIOR HIGH SCHOOL

Children in early adolescence pose particular problems for educators. They are at a transitional stage when important changes are taking place in their intellectual and social development — changes that are often reflected in a decline in academic performance and the development of negative attitudes toward school. Educators disagree whether the youngsters in the eleven-to-fourteen age group need the structure of the elementary grades or whether they can better thrive in the greater freedom of the high school environment.

We believe that junior high school has been the neglected alleyway of education reform. Yet experts on the American school system know that junior high schools are where the foundations for poor high school performance are established. With the knowledge currently available, it is difficult to judge whether the institution of junior high school needs structural reform or whether there should be a new focus on the special educational needs and problems of the age group that attends these schools. **We believe that junior high and middle schools — and the children who attend them — should be a major focus of education reform. But before successful reform can be implemented, they should become the focus of new educational research and scrutiny.**

The results of a wide range of examinations given to elementary and junior high school students over the years yield a significant paradox: Elementary school test scores are improving for low-achieving students, but we do not observe the same improvement in the junior high school. What is happening between elementary and junior high school? The answer may lie in the fact that elementary school tests measure the student's ability to do simple arithmetic operations and to decode words on a page. At the junior high school level, the tests begin to probe for more complex kinds of skills related to comprehension, understanding, and analysis. The junior high school is where the foundations for problem-solving skills must be firmly established, and the fact that this is not happening to the degree that it should may account for the declining achievement of those at the upper end of the achievement scale. In addition, junior high is the point at which lower achievers internalize negative attitudes toward school and demonstrate chronically poor school performance. Teachers find that those with a high risk of dropping out of high school are fairly easy to recognize during the junior high school years.

For average and higher-achieving students, the junior high school is pivotal in setting long-term attitudes toward the study of science. According to one study, at grade three about half the students have positive attitudes toward science, by grade eight, the proportion drops to only 20 percent.[4] This may be a significant decision point for establishing who our future scientists, mathematicians, and engineers will be. This problem deserves further study, particularly as it pertains to the entry of women and minorities into these fields.

Investment Possibilities. Studies of particularly successful junior high schools suggest that schoolwide efforts are needed to raise overall achievement in these grades and that a high degree of parental involvement is essential. Better school management at this level is also badly needed. In the junior high and middle school, more than at any other level, the quality of the time spent on learning seems at least as important as the amount of time spent on task. Generally, almost no time is spent in junior high school classrooms on developing problem-solving skills, although this is the age at which such skills should be firmly established in preparation for the more demanding work of high school.

One of the difficulties of improving achievement in the middle grades is the unsettled nature of young adolescents, who are entering a period of great uncertainty in their lives. Some of the most successful programs at this level carefully combine instructional and social service activities. Cities in Schools is a national dropout prevention program that brings teams of social service professionals into individual schools to work in a systematic way with the children identified by their school principal as most at risk. By far the largest proportion of Cities in Schools programs is based in junior high schools, although in some communities they are reaching down into the elementary school to provide similar services. Programs operate in such diverse cities as New York, Atlanta, Houston, and West Palm Beach, Florida.

Another recent effort aimed specifically at junior high schools is an endowment of $1 million created by the John Hancock Mutual Life Insurance Company for use in twenty-two middle schools in Boston. The funds are earmarked for a broad range of innovative academic and intramural athletic programs. Participation by students in the athletic portion of the program will depend upon their meeting attendance and classroom standards set by the superintendent.

---

4. National Academy of Sciences and National Academy of Engineering, *Science and Mathematics in the Schools: Report of a Convocation* (Washington, D.C.: National Academy Press, 1982).

HIGH SCHOOL PERFORMANCE

Most of the recent reports and studies on educational quality concentrate almost exclusively on improving standards and requirements in the high schools. The implication is that whatever is wrong with American education resides in the high schools and can be fixed at that level. We disagree. The high schools, in fact, exercise little quality control over the achievement levels of their entering students. This is not an argument for letting high schools off the hook; but it suggests that in our zeal to find an easily reformable target, we should not be putting all the blame on the last stage of the process.

Performance of Low Achievers. Although the average student is generally doing acceptably well in high school (at least in terms of the current job market), the real problems in high school achievement seem to be at both the upper and lower ends of the spectrum.

The lowest achievers and those who drop out have the highest risk of not being able to find a suitable place in the job market. Such young people are most likely to have serious employment problems if they come from poor families, live in poverty areas, live where the mix of jobs is such that few youths are employed, and have no older relations to recommend them for a job. Being black seems to compound all of these impediments. Additional hurdles confront teenage mothers; they are far more likely to cut short their education, have larger families, and become permanently locked out of the labor market.

A 1978 CED study of the hard-to-employ examined how the serious weakness in the school-to-work transition contributes to reduced employment opportunities for this group of students. The report concluded that many low-achieving students and dropouts never learn the basic skills and work-related behaviors that are necessary for success on the job. As a consequence, these youths have fewer opportunities for employment, and even if employed, they are less productive and adaptable. Among its recommendations, the CED report on the hard-to-employ urged schools to improve the school-to-work transition by making greater use of programs that provide outside work experience related to classroom learning.[5]

As yet, the schools seem to have done little to improve the prospects of these low achievers but they cannot bear sole blame for these problems; the causes are many and run very deep. Nevertheless, we believe that there is much that the schools can do to prepare these students better for the job markets in which they will find themselves.

Time and again, research demonstrates that these students are served

---

5. For a more complete discussion of the problems of youth unemployment see *Jobs for the Hard-to-Employ: New Directions for a Public-Private Partnership* (New York: Committee for Economic Development, 1978), pp. 52–59.

best by programs that combine work experience with education. The work-school combination for many of these high-risk students provides an important motivational force. It teaches them about working, helps them to earn extra money, and shows that they can be successful on the job.

We recommend that schools work with local businesses to design and implement better work-study and/or cooperative education programs, and that state and local governments assign these programs a high priority in policy and financing decisions. However, as we noted in Chapter 2, high school vocational education programs that do not teach specific job skills have not been successful either in terms of providing good remedial education or adequate employability skills and do not provide necessary compensatory education.

Helping Dropouts. Residential vocational programs do seem to provide good compensatory help for students who have already dropped out of the educational system. The most successful program of this type has been the Job Corps, in which boarding schools provide a mixture of skills training, remedial education, improved motivation, and health care. Because the costs of the Job Corps are considered high, it has received more careful evaluation than almost any other employment and training program.[6] The benefits to participants in the form of increased earnings are on average extremely high, and the rate of return to society is also high. From the point of view of taxpayers, this program is almost costless in the long run if the benefits of reduced criminal activities, reduced welfare payments, and higher tax contributions by higher earning corps graduates are taken into consideration. **We urge federal, state, and local authorities to continue to fund an adequate Job Corps program in areas where there is a significantly high dropout rate.**

High Achievers. The problem among the group of students at the highest end of the achievement scale has been the acute and alarming decline in higher-order analytical skills over the past two decades. The evidence from the NAEP confirms a decline in higher-level skills for seventeen-year-olds still in school. An NAEP survey, covering the period from 1970 to 1980, found that only 5 to 10 percent of these students showed strong analytical skills, and only 31 percent could correctly perform a simple inferential comprehension exercise. Furthermore, only 15 percent could write persuasively, which represented a 25 percent decline in that skill between 1974 and 1979. Similar weaknesses were also displayed in mathematical problem solving.[7]

---

6. Charles Mallar, Stuart Kerachsky, Craig Thornton, and David Long, *Evaluation of the Economic Impact of the Job Corps Program: Third Follow-Up Report* (Princeton, N.J.: Mathematica Policy Research, Inc., September 1982).

---

7. "The Information Society: Are High School Graduates Ready?" (Denver: Education Commission of the States, 1982).

Traditional teaching techniques are highly effective for developing problem-solving skills, but they are necessarily labor intensive, requiring high-quality teachers with high standards, expectations, and demands. We deal with the question of improving the performance of teachers in Chapter 4.

In fact, high school may not be the optimal place for developing problem-solving and analytical skills. Research on child development makes it increasingly clear that the foundations for these skills should be established at an earlier age and that once the developmental opportunities are passed, it is difficult to regain lost ground.

EDUCATION RESEARCH

Private industry could not succeed with a data collection system and research base as weak as this nation has in the field of education. Yet, it is only through education research and data collection that we can expect to identify ways and means to increase the output of the educational system. The original purpose of a federal role in education was as a national repository of information, and the first federal Department of Education, launched in the 1860s, was designed to accomplish that objective.

We believe that increased productivity in education over the long term will stem mainly from the application of high-quality education research. Accordingly, we recommend that the federal government increase the quality and relevance of its education research and data collection through the Department of Education and those organizations with which it works.

There are several specific areas that warrant improved data collection and analysis.

■ **Comparative Data on Educational Achievement.** Educators, parents, and policy makers should have readily available to them the statistical information that will permit state-by-state, city-by-city, and school-by-school comparisons. It is only through the use of such comparative data that deficiencies and successes can be revealed and actions mapped out according to need.

■ **Adult Deficiencies.** In light of the unacceptable level of functional illiteracy among large numbers of the adult population, federal education data collection and analysis activities should include dropouts and adults who are not now in school.

■ **Employment Readiness.** Regular assessments of employment needs enable us to learn a great deal about preparation for employment. **We believe that it would be helpful if every four years there were an assessment of the employment needs of business and the employment readiness of high school graduates designed by an advisory committee with substan-**

tial representation from the business community. Funding could be provided by Congress through appropriations for the NAEP from discretionary funds available to the Department of Labor under the Jobs Training and Partnership Act (JTPA) or from the Department of Education under the Vocational Education Act. In regard to the latter, we note that such an assessment would be in accord with the requirement in the 1984 reauthorization that calls for a national assessment of vocational education.

■ **International Comparisons.** The long-term economic and educational health of the nation depends in part on a clear understanding of both what our industrial competitors are doing and how well they are doing it. International data collection and comparative analysis are still in their infancy. At a minimum, such comparisons should be available on a regular basis for the OECD countries; ideally, we should be able to have useful data from Eastern Bloc countries and less developed nations as well.

■ **Educational Technology.** The application to education of computers and other technologies has the potential for bringing about a revolution in the way teachers teach, the way children learn, and the way schools are managed. Development in applicable technologies should be carefully monitored by the Department of Education and the appropriate research agencies. Several major national studies of this technology issue are currently underway, and the results of this research will have to be carefully evaluated by national and local policy makers before the resulting policy implications can be put into practice effectively.

One of the most important education research organizations is the NAEP, which was created in 1969 to collect and report information about the knowledge, skills, and attitudes of nine-, thirteen-, and seventeen-year-olds in writing, reading, mathematics, science, literature, art, music, social studies, computer competence, citizenship, and career and occupational development. It is funded by the National Institute of Education, the research arm of the Department of Education, and administered by the Educational Testing Service (ETS). In addition to reporting on national educational achievement by age group, the NAEP has begun to provide information by grade level (third, seventh, and eleventh) as well. We support this strengthening of the NAEP as essential for providing the nation with better and more accurate information on the nation's schools.

LONGER SCHOOL DAY AND YEAR

A number of experts have suggested reorganizing the public schools on a year-round model as another way to improve the cost-effectiveness of education. The rationale for year-round schools is threefold: first, increasing time-on-task has been shown to increase learning retention; second, year-round schooling would help two-career families and single parents avoid complicated child-care arrangements during the long summer; and third, a year-round model may help bring teachers' salaries in line with other professions and provide greater opportunites for professional growth.

Currently, few communities have tried this approach, and there is, as yet, no way to assess whether lengthening the school day or year or having school operate on a year-round schedule would be cost-effective on a national basis. However, Los Angeles and Houston are experimenting with the year-round concept, and they have had some promising results.

In Los Angeles, more than ninety of the 600 public schools are currently operating on a year-round basis, although only a handful of students attend school all year. This program is a response to what would otherwise be unmanageable overcrowding of school facilities. Students are grouped into four clusters, three of which are in the building at any one time. In between every nine-week session, each cluster gets a three-week vacation. Teachers still operate on a thirty-six-week contract, but they have the option of signing up as substitute teachers for an additional twelve-week assignment, earning extra pay in the process. Although summer school is available, most children do not attend all four sessions.

Houston also experimented successfully with a year-round school and found that those students who attended this school had markedly higher achievement test scores. As a consequence, Houston has extended its original single-school program to thirteen additional schools.

One of the arguments in favor of year-round schools, that the loss in learning retention which takes place over a long summer vacation may be kept to a minimum with year-round operation, may be bolstered by the experiment in Houston. Other arguments include making more efficient use of school facilities and support personnel, being able to pay teachers and other personnel higher salaries commensurate with the greater amount of time they work, permitting more flexible promotion policies for youngsters who do not meet increased standards during their normal attendance time, and providing more and better day-care for the children of working parents, for whom the long summer vacation often presents a major logistical problem. What year-round schools could mean for teachers professionally is discussed in more detail in Chapter 4.

FINANCING EDUCATION

Investments in education need to be made in the context of complicated state, local, and federal financing arrangements. By any measure, American education is big business. But if we examine where our current

WITHDRAWN
SCCCC - LIBRARY
4601 Mid Rivers Mall Drive
St. Peters, MO 63376

educational expenditures are being channeled, a confusing picture emerges. In 1983, the nation spent nearly $130 billion on public elementary and secondary schools, which amounts to an average of $3,200 per child. At 3.9 percent of gross national product, education is second only to health care as the nation's largest service industry. Between 1970 and 1980, total expenditures for elementary and secondary public education rose 12.3 percent, in constant dollars, even though enrollments declined by over 10 percent. However, the entire increase was channeled to noninstructional purposes. The amount spent on teacher salaries in public schools, as a percentage of total expenditures, actually declined almost 10 percent in that decade, from 48 percent in 1970 to 38.5 percent in 1980.

Because education is primarily funded on the state and local levels, resources available for education vary considerably from state to state and from community to community. Obviously, there are some states and localities, particularly "model" suburban communities, such as Scarsdale in New York State and Highland Park outside of Chicago, that are well-endowed with both human and financial resources and have consistently led the nation in educational achievement.

But many more school districts, particularly those in older urban areas, ports-of-entry for new immigrants, and rural communities, are in need of a greater level of financial investment than they are currently receiving. These are often the same areas that are now having difficult times economically. Therefore, it is all the more important for state and local authorities to weigh very carefully the various reform strategies we propose and to judge which educational investments will provide the best returns for their students.

Both the public and the business community have let it be known that they would be willing to spend more on education if reforms are designed to improve educational quality and can be shown to yield results. In almost every state, the business community is participating to some degree in efforts to upgrade the public school system. For example, the California Roundtable, an association of business leaders, has worked closely with the State Superintendent of Public Instruction, the governor, and legislative leaders to design a sweeping education reform package, and has helped to ensure that program's passage through the state legislature. In Arkansas, a citizens committee, working closely with business leaders and the governor, has helped to implement a program of education reforms designed to bring that state's schools up to competitive national standards. Like its California counterpart, the Minnesota Business Partnership commissioned a major study of elementary and secondary education in that state and its members have been working closely with state policy makers to build consensus on the need for fundamentally restructuring Minnesota's educational system.

WHO CONTROLS EDUCATIONAL SPENDING?

For the most part, state governments provide the largest share of educational funds, and local school districts provide the rest. The federal government provides less than 7 percent of total elementary and secondary public school funding, although this varies somewhat from state to state. This federal role is vital; most of the funds it provides are targeted to compensatory and remedial education. However, the major share of any new educational funds is most likely to come from state sources and, to some extent, from local communities.

On the local level, property taxes are the best-known source of funds for education. However, with states assuming more of the responsibility for directly providing operating revenues for the schools, the importance of property taxes is gradually declining, and states are shifting to heavier reli-

WHO FUNDS EDUCATION?

How It Has Changed: 1970 and 1984

(by source of funds in current dollars)

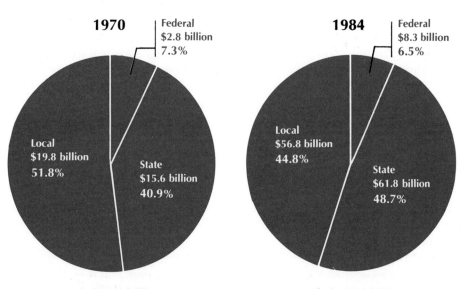

1970

Federal
$2.8 billion
7.3%

Local
$19.8 billion
51.8%

State
$15.6 billion
40.9%

Total: $38.2 billion

1984

Federal
$8.3 billion
6.5%

Local
$56.8 billion
44.8%

State
$61.8 billion
48.7%

Total: $126.9 billion

SOURCE: Statistical Abstract of The United States, 1985, p. 143.

ance on broadly based taxes on sales, use, and income. Increasingly, dedicated revenue sources imposed at the state level are being tied to education; most common are so-called sin taxes on alcohol, tobacco, and lottery or gambling proceeds.

FEDERAL ROLE

The distribution of federal funds for public elementary and secondary education varies widely. For example, federal funds account for less than 3 percent of total expenditures in Minnesota and Wisconsin, but more than 20 percent in Mississippi. Overwhelmingly, most of the federal funds are directed toward special populations and programs that foster equal access and opportunity, such as those for the disadvantaged, the handicapped, and women.

The federal government has assumed a long-term responsibility for meeting the special educational needs of minorities, the handicapped, and women, and it should assure that this responsibility is being met. But it is now time for states and localities to assume a larger role in meeting their obligations to these groups.

STATE ROLE

So far during the 1980s, state governments have provided the major share of new educational revenues. Of the total increase in funding between 1981 and 1983, $12 billion, or 56 percent, came from state sources.[8] The figure on page 55 describes how dramatically the distribution of state, local, and federal funds changed between 1970 and 1984.

Although in 1984 states provided an average of 48.7 percent of school revenues and localities provided an average of 44.8 percent, there is considerable variation in the ratio of state to local expenditures from state to state. Exclusive of federal funds, over 90 percent of school revenue in New Hampshire is generated locally through the property tax, while in Hawaii 100 percent of school costs are borne by the state. As a consequence of Proposition 13, California changed its ratio of state-to-local funding dramatically. In 1972, exclusive of federal funds, 38 percent of school costs in California were borne by the state; by 1984, the proportion had climbed to 74 percent.

This tendency for state government to become the senior partner in the funding of education can have both positive and negative results. On the positive side, state control of education dollars may result in more equitable distribution of resources among rich and poor districts. At the same time, greater state control of education funding has spurred a tendency toward

---

8. Allen Odden, "Financing Educational Excellence." Unpublished paper prepared for the Committee for Economic Development's Subcommittee on Business and the Schools, 1983.

larger bureaucracies and greater centralization of education decison making. In most states, there are formal state restrictions on how local funds can be used, and states have tended to exert control over local school districts in rough proportion to the level of state funds provided. In the face of their growing role in education, state governments are likely to continue to increase their control over local school districts.

In accordance with the principles of bottom-up management, we are strongly opposed to the trend toward increased centralization of decision-making power at the state level. We believe that even as the states assume more of the burden of financing local schools, they must resist the impulse to run the schools. **We favor state standard-setting as a necessary and appropriate accompaniment to state financial support, but not state management or control of local schools.**

However, we also believe that state educational authorities can provide guidance and support for local schools by careful application of proven business management practices, such as those discussed in Chapter 2. For example, if a school, or school system, is declared educationally bankrupt, the state authorities should be responsible for seeing that it is brought up to standard. Similarly, states can reward some of their most promising schools by easing prescriptive regulations so that they can design programs that best meet their specific educational objectives.

We also believe that the power to raise and allocate funds should not reside exclusively at the state level. **Although states should be responsible for seeing to it that all local systems have sufficient resources to ensure the essential elements of a satisfactory school program, state finance formulas should also specifically provide local communities with the authority and the incentives to raise funds and make spending decisions at the district level.**

LOCAL ROLE

Successful corporations delegate authority and responsibility to their organizational units because that is where expertise and insight can best be brought to bear. Failure to delegate robs lower echelons of initiative, leads to excessive bureaucratization, and stifles creativity.

Similarly, we are convinced that higher levels of government are not better able to make sensitive and sensible education decisions than those that deal with the schools from day to day. Despite the trend toward more state funding and control, local school boards, administrators, teachers, and parents are more sophisticated about the processes of education today than at any other time in our history. There is sound evidence that decisions about school organization and management are best made at the local level. Like effective businesses, effective schools should be able to set targets, have well-defined goals and objectives, and measure their accomplishment without higher levels of management dictating how those objectives should be met. However, if schools do not achieve their objectives or perform up to the standards set, state and local education authorities should be able to intervene to provide direct supervision or to reorganize the school. **We remain convinced of the value of local control in American public education, and the bottom-up approach to school reform that we advocate is founded on that concept. Accordingly, we recommend that school governance be retained at the local level and that it not be supplanted by statewide boards of education.**

The principal job of local school boards and managers is to make tough allocation decisions and establish priorities. **We recommend that local boards of education should do a better job of identifying priorities, budgeting for them accordingly, and performing only those tasks for which funding is available. In the event that local boards are improperly constrained by federal or state rules, regulations, or statutes, we recommend that business work with the local school boards to lobby state and federal legislatures for relief.**

BUSINESS ROLE

Financing public education is a public responsibility through local, state, and federal mechanisms. Business should not be in the position of financing public education in any substantial way except as a taxpayer. It would serve the interests of neither business nor education for corporations to attempt to provide a major portion of local school funds out of business profits.

In Chapter 5, we discuss in detail the many ways in which business can become involved with schools and school systems through partnerships and other collaborative activities. These will never represent a major source of funds for the schools, nor should they. However, business should be prepared to shoulder its fair share of the burden for education, including taxes and active support for better schools. Moreover, business leaders have shown time and again that they are willing to use their influence in support of larger school budgets when there is evidence that such support will produce better-educated students.

CHAPTER 4

TEACHERS AND SCHOOLS

It is traditional wisdom in the business world that a corporation is only as good as the people it employs. Similarly, our schools can be no better than the teachers who staff them.

This Committee believes that improvements in the quality of teaching must come from enhancing and strengthening the professional roles of teachers, maximizing their abilities and opportunities to exercise judgment and make decisions, and reshaping and upgrading their working environments. Such actions, together with measures designed to assure high standards and competitive salaries and to encourage community and parent support, can help to attract and retain highly qualified people and improve the effectiveness of the entire profession.

At the same time, we want to underscore an essential prerequisite for reform: *None of these improvements can be made without strengthening school management and leadership.*

Neither the schools nor the teaching profession will benefit from policies designed to compensate for or accommodate unqualified teachers. Nor will they gain from "teacher-proof" materials or from evaluation systems that focus on technical practices rather than on performance and initiative. In contrast, our strategy for improving teaching focuses on increasing the professional abilities of teachers and broadening their decision-making role in the educational process. It recognizes *the school building* as the place where changes have to be made and implemented.

In sum, we are calling for nothing less than a revolution in the role of the teacher and the management of the schools. We are convinced that comprehensive reform is necessary in order to achieve any significant upgrading in the quality of teaching and the performance of our public schools. We are aware that such a strategy places heavy demands on legislatures, on the colleges and universities that prepare teachers, on state and local education agencies, on superintendents and principals, and especially on teachers and teacher organizations.

Our recommendations are interrelated. For example, to raise teachers' salaries, without making the necessary changes in standards, teaching conditions, and the education and training of teachers is not likely to improve the quality of teaching substantially. Therefore, the recommendations presented in this chapter need to be carried out concurrently rather than piecemeal.

A PROBLEM
AND AN OPPORTUNITY

In previous generations the ranks of teachers were filled with many highly qualified people who for various reasons viewed the profession either as desirable or as their only option. Among them were casualties of the 1930s, some of whom were trained for other professions but could find employment only in the schools, and post-Depression college graduates seeking the job security of a teaching position. For women and minorities, teaching was one of very few career options. Those from rural areas and second-generation immigrants were also drawn to teaching, viewing it as a step upward on the occupational ladder. In the 1960s, the teacher work force benefited from those who chose teaching over the draft. The result of all these circumstances was to seed the schools with educated and talented individuals.

Today such motivations either no longer exist or do not operate as forcefully. The schools, like most other institutions, must now compete primarily on the basis of market forces. However, the schools' ability to compete in the market has been further eroded by the decline in both the absolute and the relative levels of teachers' pay. In absolute terms, the purchasing power of the average teacher's pay has declined 15 percent since 1973.

Historically, teachers' salaries have always been relatively low and the conditions of teaching less than ideal. In other times, these factors were either overlooked or accepted because of the personal satisfaction of teaching and its respected status in the community.

This is no longer the case. Competent people, including women and minorities, can now choose other occupations, and the public no longer holds teaching in high regard. In 1969, 75 percent of Gallup survey respondents indicated they would like a child of theirs to pursue teaching as a career; in 1984, only 45 percent gave this answer. In answering why they felt negatively about teaching they mentioned, in order of frequency: low pay, discipline problems, thankless work, and low prestige.[1] Another factor that is clearly linked to the status of teaching is the perception that teachers lack effectiveness.

Although the portion of the labor market that provided teaching candidates was diverted to more prestigious, higher paying occupations, the schools changed, too. Especially in the large urban districts, they have become highly bureaucratic, and the school population has expanded to include students who formerly would have left before graduation. For teachers, such changes have produced added difficulties.

DECLINE IN TEACHER QUALITY

Where a sex differential once operated, a quality differential now determines who becomes a teacher. In the past few years, qualifications of those entering teaching have declined. The SAT scores of college-bound students who identify teaching as their prospective profession have consistently been lower than those of students entering other professions or graduate training programs (see figure, page 63). Although there has been an overall decline in SAT scores within the last decade, new teacher candidates' scores have dipped even lower. In addition, it is the most academically able teachers who are the first to leave the profession. A study of attrition rates of teachers in North Carolina indicated that two-thirds of the teachers who scored in the top 10 percent of the National Teacher Examination had left teaching within seven years.[2]

---

1. "The 15th Annual Gallup Poll of the Public's Attitude Toward the Public Schools," *Phi Delta Kappan*, 1984, pp. 33–47.

---

2. Phillip C. Schlechty and Victor S. Vance, "Do Academically Able Teachers Leave Education? The North Carolina Case," *Phi Delta Kappan*, Vol. 63, 1981, pp. 106–112.

QUANTITATIVE GAPS

The decline in academic ability of education students has been taking place for some time but its full impact has not yet been felt. That is about to change. Over the past decade, there has been a 10 percent decline in elementary and secondary school enrollments. Because teacher turnover has been steady at about 6 percent, there has been relatively little demand for new teachers; this has had a stabilizing effect on the teaching population.

As the teacher work force becomes older, and with fewer new teachers added over the past decade, expected retirements will thin the teaching ranks. At the same time, the school-age population is expected to grow by approximately 10 percent over the next 15 years. Projections indicate extensive teacher shortages by 1992, with continuing severe shortages in certain subjects, such as science and mathematics (see figure, page 63).

If no changes are made to turn teaching into a more attractive profession, the future demand for teachers will mean that vacancies will increasingly be filled with poorly qualified candidates. As shortages drive up salaries, the schools will be building a higher-paid but poorer-quality teaching force. Unless deliberate steps are taken to attract and keep quality applicants, such poorly qualified teachers will become the tenured teaching force for the next two generations. The problem, therefore, takes on critical dimensions.

WINDOW OF OPPORTUNITY

This situation may be viewed as a window of opportunity. Given the "graying" of the teacher force and steady increases in the school age population, it is estimated that about 1.3 million new teachers will be needed by 1990. Changes that are made now in the recruitment and education of new teacher candidates can affect the quality of the teaching profession for decades to come. However, if highly qualified people are attracted to teaching but compensation and working environments quickly drive them away, the schools will have gained very little. Realistically, the strength of the teaching profession will depend on our ability to attract the best people and provide the conditions, motivations, and incentives that will retain and support them as effective teachers.

IMPROVING THE TEACHING PROFESSION

If we are to take advantage of this opportunity to influence the quality of teaching, it is important to understand some of the occupational characteristics of teachers and teaching.

A teacher shortage is imminent . . .

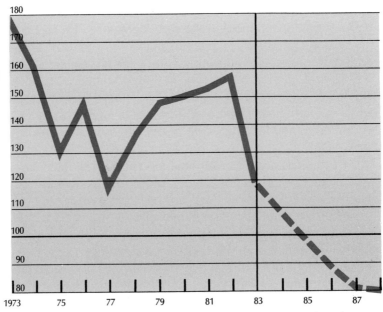

Supply of
new teachers
as a % of
the demand
for additional
teachers

. . . but the academic ability of incoming teachers has been declining.

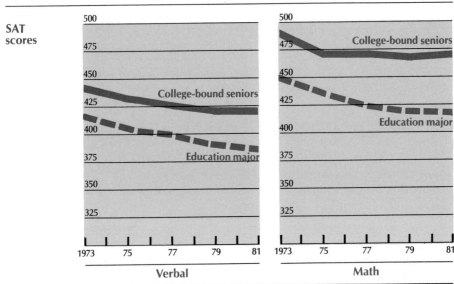

SAT
scores

Verbal

Math

SOURCE: Linda Darling-Hammond, *Beyond the Commission Reports: The Coming Crisis in Teaching* (Santa Monica, California: The Rand Corporation, 1984), pp. 2 and 7.

First, teaching historically has been predominantly a woman's occupation, and this has affected its status, compensation, and culture. Now, the changed status of women in American society has meant that many talented women have left, or never entered, the classroom in favor of higher-paying, higher-status occupations. Often overlooked is the fact that the culture, mores, and compensation patterns of teaching are now largely obsolete. If indeed they were ever appropriate, they are no longer.

Second, there is a tendency to lump together all teachers at all levels and in all geographic regions. In fact, there are important differences between elementary and secondary teachers, and there is great diversity among states and localities with respect to prevailing problems and conditions.

Third, real career opportunities and good working conditions are powerful magnets for attracting and retaining good people and supporting their effectiveness.

In order to have a cumulative effect, proposals for reform must be based on a consistent definition of teaching quality. We view teaching as a profession, and our recommendations have been developed to enhance and support the professional roles of teachers. Taking advantage of the window of opportunity will require that schools compete actively in the labor market. Public education will have to become a more competitive employer. If it does not, it will not be able to attract or retain quality candidates.

TEACHER COMPENSATION

Low salaries are frequently identified as a major cause of teacher dissatisfaction. Entry-level salaries for teachers are low, and what is more important, they are noncompetitive. The average starting salary for teachers in the 1984–1985 period was estimated at $15,394, much lower than the average for other beginning professionals with a college degree. The problem becomes even more acute as teaching salaries drop farther behind other professional salaries in the course of a career.

Although low starting salaries and low pay ceilings generally characterize teaching, there is a very broad range within the profession. When benefits are taken into consideration, the range is even broader. In fact, when one compares averages among the states, the highest salary is more than twice as much as the lowest.[3]

We recognize that some of the budget constraints common to all pub-

---

3. C. Emily Feistritzer, *The Conditions of Teaching* (Princeton: Carnegie Foundation for the Advancement of Teaching, 1983).

lic-sector employment will have to be applied to the salary structure of teachers. Salary is generally not the primary reason most teachers enter the profession; job satisfaction is. However, the continuing decline in the compensation of teaching, compared to other professions that require similar background and training, coupled with generally unsatisfactory working conditions, has led to a point of diminishing returns for prospective teachers. Indeed, even if the conditions under which most teachers labor were to improve substantially, current salaries would still be too low to attract the kind of top-quality, dedicated individuals that teaching needs.

We believe that effective compensation plans can achieve at least three objectives that are central to improving the quality of teaching:

- More competitive entry-level salaries can attract better-qualified people into teaching.

- Attractive opportunities linked to pay progression can help retain such people as career professionals.

- A well-designed plan linking pay to performance can both stimulate professional interaction and encourage and reward excellence in teaching.

ENTRY-LEVEL SALARIES

We recommend increased salaries for both entry-level and career teachers in order to attract high-quality individuals into the profession. Those responsible for establishing teacher salaries at the local level should examine the salaries of other occupations requiring similar education and training and should identify those fields and occupations that teachers enter when leaving education. In practically every major community, the business community conducts a salary survey to determine average salary levels by occupation. Local school boards should participate in these surveys.

Entry-level salaries may attract people into teaching, but it is the career salary structure that contributes substantially to the choice of profession. Moreover, entry-level salaries neither reward quality nor improve it. Alternative compensation plans are needed to address those issues.

LINKING SALARIES TO RESPONSIBILITY

The work of most teachers is essentially the same from the first day until retirement. A professional path for teachers would satisfy the need to attract career-oriented people and serve as a basis for differentiating salaries. Moreover, well-designed career ladders can provide for the needed definition of teaching roles, allow teachers to choose to develop their abilities in a variety of ways, provide for the professional mentoring needed for new teachers, and create a solid structure for increasing the professionalism of teaching.

Career ladders should be grounded in the role of the teacher as a professional educator; they should not be based on increasing levels of administrative responsibility. The general lack of a career path in teaching has deep roots in the development of a profession characterized by high turnover and a predominance of women with short or interrupted careers. From a competitive standpoint, such an occupation is far less desirable today than it may have been in the past. Moreover, this single-stage structure has often resulted in the departure of highly motivated teachers into administration in order to achieve increases in salary and status. We believe there should be enough flexibility in teaching to attract both people who are interested in the traditional career and those who want to move up a career ladder or enter administration.

Reforms must be designed to link pay to responsibility. Here are two examples.

■ **Master teacher plans.** An occupational hierarchy can be created with several levels through which teachers pass on the basis of demonstrated competence, experience, and career development. Different responsibilities are associated with each level. Some plans are based on voluntary participation; others act as selective screens, requiring teachers to move up or out until at least midlevel career status is reached. At that stage, participation becomes voluntary. These master teacher plans may be developed statewide or for local districts. State plans are being designed in California, Florida, Tennessee, and other states. The Charlotte-Mecklenburg Plan in North Carolina represents a local school district design (see page 73).

■ **Full-year teaching model.** Teachers now working on ten-month contracts could be moved up to full-year status — twelve-month contracts, with vacation set minimally at two weeks and increasing to four weeks with seniority. How this might tie into the year-round school model is examined in Chapter 3. For teachers, this additional time would be used for school-oriented activities and professional development. If teacher time were increased 15 percent with a commensurate increase in salary, and if such time were spent in productive professional interchange, it would allow the teacher to focus more sharply on educational content during the rest of the year. It is not unreasonable, therefore, to expect measurable gains in student performance. Indeed, some of this time should be spent in developing the skills of new teachers. The full-year teaching model would not take the place of a master teacher plan, although some school districts might want to combine the two.

Reliable financial support is critical for such changes to be effective. There are also likely to be considerable opportunities for funding as the nation experiences teacher shortages in certain areas. Some portion of these resources should be set aside for career ladders and staff development; not all salary money should be used simply to increase the size of the teacher work force. In addition, state programs should consider equity issues relating to the funding abilities of their local school districts in order to avoid a situation in which some districts may have a full complement of master teachers while others are unable to afford them.

LINKING PAY TO PERFORMANCE

At present, few formulas exist for rewarding outstanding teachers. Rewarding outstanding performance is to be encouraged, but it is not clear what impact such financial incentives will have on improving the overall quality of teaching, especially if poor performance is the result of low ability, inadequate training, or unsatisfactory working conditions. For some teachers, financial incentives will provide the added motivation to improve performance; for others, there will be no improvement unless other changes are made.

Merit pay programs award additional funds to teachers on the basis of periodic evaluation of the teachers' performance, the students' performance, or both. Merit pay may take the form of permanent salary increases or of annual bonuses for excellent teachers.

Individual merit pay schemes that limit the number of teachers who may participate are likely to have a negative effect on the collegial relationship of the faculty. Teachers working in a largely competitive environment will be less inclined to share or to encourage and support the feeling of community that is clearly associated with effective schools. A number of school systems that have adopted merit pay have dropped the system because of administrative difficulties, low morale, staff dissension, and financial difficulties.[4]

The experience of business with merit pay points to another significant problem: Although it is relatively easy to identify the highest and lowest performers in an organization, evaluation decisions for the wide middle range are far more difficult. Moreover, the performance of those in the middle is also likely to be affected by an individual merit pay plan.

Despite the poor track record of current merit pay schemes that are linked to individual performance, we believe that it is important to continue to experiment with model programs that both reward individual excellence and encourage increased cooperation and collegial interaction among a

---

4. Glen Robinson, *Concerns in Education* (Arlington, Virginia: Education Research Service, May 1983), p. 3.

school's teaching staff. **We recommend that school districts experiment with alternative pay systems which would provide both annual bonus awards for a small percentage of outstanding teachers and incentives that link pay to performance on a group basis.** A bonus award would recognize outstanding performance and would be less costly because it would not be built into the salary structure. The group incentive would stimulate professional interaction and provide opportunities for middle-range teachers to learn from their peers.

We recommend that the performance base for determining both bonuses and group merit pay include a wide range of measures extending, for example, from student performance relative to ability to involvement in professional activities. Teachers should participate in the selection of the criteria that govern the performance base.

DIFFERENTIAL PAY

The compensation system for teachers can also be used to fill positions in areas where critical shortages exist, such as mathematics, science, and inner-city schools. **We recommend that school districts provide financial incentives at the levels required to attract qualified people to fill vacancies in areas where there are critical shortages.**

In our view, these compensation requirements are essential and necessary if public education is to function more competitively in the labor market. They recognize both the financial limitations of a public-sector profession and the need for teaching to move away from its outdated structure and culture toward a new definition of professionalism. But they also assume that management will provide schools with the capability of developing and supporting teachers on the job. This means a serious commitment of resources for staff development.

WORKING CONDITIONS

More professionalism and better compensation might go a long way toward attracting some highly qualified students into teaching, but what happens when these bright new teachers enter the schools and find the conditions of teaching not only difficult but also unpleasant?

There are actually two problems to be confronted in this context. The first is how to create an environment that can attract and retain highly skilled, competent people. The second is how to create an environment that motivates and supports high levels of commitment and performance from all teachers. Of course not every classroom will be filled by a superstar, but the schools can nevertheless provide environments that will attract and retain highly competent career-oriented teachers. Similarly, conditions, rewards, and incentives can be designed to encourage and support high performance, even from teachers of average ability.

Moreover, there are aspects of the schools apart from those involving teachers that can improve the attitudes of people who work in the system and strengthen their performance. These include the cleanliness and maintenance of buildings and other amenities associated with the modern working world.

In many respects, times have changed but schools have not. The rapid growth of population and public schooling encouraged schools to grow in a cellular fashion. Classrooms and teachers were added as needed. This structure reinforced isolated teaching and presented barriers to the development of a sense of community in school buildings. Because women made up most of the teacher work force, the norms of the larger society governing their behavior and occupational roles came to dominate the teaching profession.

There has also been a change in the work of teaching. Recent decades have heaped responsibilities on the schools that far exceed the expertise or control of the classroom teacher. Teachers are expected to diagnose and deal with special education needs, social and family change affecting student performance, and a general decline in parental control and involvement. These are appropriate roles for teachers, and their compensation should reflect their responsibilities.* However, teachers are also burdened with clerical and housekeeping chores which detract from their performance as professional educators.

One obvious remedy to the problem of working conditions is to reduce these nonprofessional responsibilities. **We recommend that the nonprofessional clerical and housekeeping responsibilities associated with teaching be sharply curtailed in order to allow teachers to perform their roles as educators better.** But this is only a partial remedy. School administrators need to create the organizational environment and provide the leadership that will support and encourage effective professional practice.

CHANGING THE ORGANIZATIONAL ENVIRONMENT

The literature on excellence in both business and school organizations highlights the importance of giving the individual school and the individual teacher genuine responsibility for the process of education. We believe that lessons derived from the experience of both education and business can be successfully applied to the organization of the schools in the areas of size, structure, staff development, evaluating career ladders, rewards and incentives, and removal of barriers.

---

*See memorandum by ROBERT W. LUNDEEN (page 103).

Size. What appears to be more important than actual size of a school or business is the ability of the leadership to create a sense of community within the organization. Through structure and management, the organization's leaders must be able to make the individual feel responsible, part of the community of shared values, and part of the whole. This may be easier to achieve in small organizations, but it is by no means limited to them.

Structure. Giving teachers a larger voice in decisions at the district and school-building levels, combined with the clear need for improving standards, will inevitably produce a certain tension. **School objectives should be tightly connected with goals established by the state, but individual schools should be given autonomy in implementing programs that meet those goals.**

The people in each school building must participate in defining the implementation process in order to feel a sense of ownership. Although leadership and encouragement from the top down are important, the goals of the school, the performance measures, and the instructional program need to be clearly articulated and coupled with the goals of individual teachers and administrators. Teachers should be allowed to exercise professional judgment in the implementation of programs, to experiment and develop instructional strategies, and to develop curriculum.

The instructional program in the school should be organized to support the interaction of teachers and to encourage a view of teaching as shared work.

Staff Development. Staff development should be designed to improve teaching and should grow out of the needs of the teachers and of the school. Salary increments for staff development should be given for activities related to increasing the effectiveness of the teacher and the school. In order for staff development to contribute to a change in the school's culture, it must focus on teacher behavior, attitudes, and expectations, as well as on developing specific teaching skills. This implies that the process used in staff development is as important as the content.

One successful technique, peer teaching, is embodied in the concept of the "teacher center," in which teachers teach teachers. Very popular in Japan, teacher centers involve groups of peers who work on problems and issues in schools, analogous to quality circles in industry. They can provide a structure for the expansion of the teacher's role from one of an isolated classroom practitioner to one of a participant in a schoolwide and school-based process. Unfortunately, teacher centers have lost financial support in this country. **We believe that teacher centers have promise for enriching and expanding the professionalism of teachers. They should be revived and encouraged.**

Evaluations. Evaluation can be a barrier to change within a school, or it can create a climate conducive to innovation and improvement.

A major study of teacher evaluation in American schools has found that most evaluation processes contribute very little to the development of the skills, behaviors, or collegial relationships so important to effective teaching.[5] In fact, the evaluation methods used by most schools relate primarily to such major steps in a teacher's career as contract renewal, tenure, or dismissal.

We believe that school systems should reexamine their evaluation methods and their assumptions regarding teacher roles and the organization and operation of schools. Evaluations that encourage individual growth and development as well as collegial relationships would go far toward improving the professionalism of teaching. Accordingly, we propose that teacher evaluations should contain the following elements:[6]

■ They should build teacher effectiveness by stressing innovation in the classroom, professional autonomy, decision-making ability, and collegial interaction.

■ They should be tied to a reward system that includes recognition of professional excellence but which does not increase teacher isolation or reduce professional collegiality.

■ They should be based on a professional definition of teaching, which includes not only the expectation that a teacher has mastered the content of his or her subject and the necessary professional skills, but which includes the expectation that a teacher will exercise professional judgment in making decisions and will be equipped to diagnose needs, prescribe solutions, and evaluate the growth and performance of students.

In addition, we suggest a two-tier system of evaluations. The first, and more traditional, would be used as the basis for decisions on contract renewal, tenure, or dismissal. These could continue to be done by a group from the district, outside the school itself. The second would primarily be a tool for encouraging professional growth and development, and should be carried out by those closest to the teacher — direct supervisors, master teachers, and principals.

We recommend that school systems experiment with different models for evaluation and that teachers play an active role in this process. Most important, the principal players in the process of change — teachers, administrators, and school boards — should focus their attention on deter-

---

5. Linda Darling-Hammond, Arthur E. Wise, and Sara R. Pease, "Teacher Evaluation in the Organizational Context: A Review of the Literature," *Review of Educational Research* 53 (Fall 1983): pp. 285-328.

---

6. Darling-Hammond, Wise, and Pease, "Teacher Evaluation."

mining appropriate measures and deciding what the process should be. The Toledo plan, described below, involves peer evaluation with the participation of the teachers' union and appears to be a promising alternative.

Career Ladders. Career ladders provide stages of responsibility and salary tied to competence and seniority. Some career ladder plans include internship and training for beginning teachers and the development of mentor roles and responsibilities for senior staff.

We believe that more attention to career ladders for teaching will lead to three very distinct and desirable outcomes.

First, a better defined career hierarchy will attract better-qualified, career-oriented people. It also can provide rewards and incentives for the classroom-oriented teacher who prefers the traditional ten-month calendar. Second, career ladders offer incentives for good performance, resulting in greater effort, ambition, and recognition. Finally, the hierarchies developed

---

THE TOLEDO PLAN

In their study of teacher evaluation,* scholars at the Rand Corporation identified certain features that districts with effective evaluation practices have in common. First and foremost, these districts took evaluation seriously and budgeted time for the process.

The Toledo Plan is an example of how a teachers organization, in this instance the Toledo (Ohio) Federation of Teachers, can assume leadership in defining and enforcing standards of professional conduct and competence.

The Toledo Plan is distinctive in two important ways. It is targeted at all beginning teachers (first-year interns) and experienced teachers who have been identified by both their principal and the union leadership as needing better supervision. Second, it uses consulting teachers, who are released from classroom duties full- or part-time for up to three years, as the primary evaluators.

The Toledo Plan established an Intern Review Board, which is chaired alternately by the assistant superintendent for personnel and the president of the Toledo Federation of Teachers. This ensures that evaluation receives top priority and high visibility in the district. Among the board's responsibilities has been the selection of consulting teachers.

The Toledo Plan develops the professional responsibilities of teachers through their organization, and it provides needed bureaucratic and financial support to the evaluation system. It puts into effect peer consultation and clinical supervision, which is supported by the literature on effective practices in teacher evaluation.

*Arthur E. Wise, Linda Darling-Hammond, Milbrey McLaughlin, and Harriet Bernstein, *Teacher Evaluation: A Study of Effective Practices* (Washington, D.C.: Rand Corporation, June 1984), pp. 36–39.

in a career ladder have an educational purpose in that they encourage more experienced teachers to share their knowledge and expertise with their younger colleagues.

Teachers should be offered career options based on ability and experience. Career ladders should be built with a very broad view, including not only the organizational environment of schools but also staff development. This will require time because it involves a change in the culture of teaching. The Charlotte-Mecklenburg Career Development Plan in North Carolina appears to be taking this comprehensive view (see below). It is built on organizational management theory and deals with training, evaluation, compensation, rewards, and staffing. We need more such models from which we can learn.

Rewards and Incentives. Honors, mentoring roles, public recognition, and stipends for travel and study are additional rewards and incentives for outstanding teachers. So, too, are small grants and school improvement fellowships that enable teachers to enrich their classroom programs. Teachers also have a role to play in policy development. As part of their professional duties, they should be encouraged to attend meetings and participate in forums on the national, state, and local levels where they would have a voice in shaping policy.

Such rewards and incentives have a payoff both for the teacher and for

THE CHARLOTTE-MECKLENBURG PLAN

This five-step career ladder, which was developed over several years, represents a change in school culture as much as it does a career-development plan.

The plan substantially changes the structure of the teacher's career from single-stage classroom teaching, with salary increments based on longevity and credits earned, to a five-stage career ladder with variations in teachers' salaries related to changes in responsibilities and job assignments. Movement up the ladder is based on teacher choice and evaluation of teacher performance. The initial career rungs are mandatory; a teacher's ability to move up these first steps are the basis for awarding tenure, which may be granted in from three to six years.

A teacher-training program has also been developed to support the implementation of this new structure. The Charlotte-Mecklenburg Plan is based on a set of interwoven parts. It provides for training, evaluation, and teacher's preferences, and it involves basic structural changes in tenure, contracts, and job assignments. If it proves to be successful, this plan may effectively increase the professionalism of teaching by increasing responsibility, salary, and status.

the school. They give teachers status and power and increase individual commitment and a sense of ownership. They also become the traditions, myths, and symbols of the school, which help build a community of shared goals and values.

We recommend that school systems provide resources necessary for funding such rewards and incentives and that they be used to build a positive school culture.

Removing Barriers. Teachers are continually confronted with barriers of time, space, and resources, as well as barriers of attitude and expectations. For many teachers there are important physical barriers. Most teachers lack easy access to telephones. Many have no permanent classroom. Some have to share desks with other teachers. Most frequently, teachers talk about having no sanctioned time to deal with problems that arise with their classes or with individual students, to plan with other teachers, to observe other classrooms, or to visit other schools. Most important, there are no systematic ways to get constructive feedback. The cost of removing these obstructions is minimal measured against the potential benefits for school systems and the students they seek to educate.

MANAGEMENT AND LEADERSHIP

Time and again strong leadership is cited as a key reason why particular schools succeed. In effective schools, good principals know how to manage, and they consider management a vital part of their responsibility.

Principal training programs need to select and train men and women who can manage both organizational change and people while guiding the educational programs of the schools. **School systems should develop ways to identify individuals with the potential for this kind of leadership, and they should devote resources and effort to the development of leadership skills in principals. And in doing so, they should enlist the help of business.**

Some programs are now putting into practice some of the lessons learned about management and leadership in industry. For example, the National Association of Secondary School Principals has developed and tested an assessment center model based on AT&T's experience in identifying potential managers. Honeywell, Inc., has developed a management training program for the St. Louis Park, Minnesota, school system. In the District of Columbia, district school administrators attend regular IBM management training courses with the help of a consortium of other companies and financial assistance from the Edna McConnell Clark Foundation.

Before a school system can successfully apply the lessons of business to the management of the schools, three steps must be taken. First, school boards and administrators need to understand better the similarities and differences between school and business management. Second, they need to develop links between schools and businesses to identify those business policies and practices that are also appropriate for schools. Third, they need to provide resources for the identification and training of principals.

In order to capture the gains in productivity and quality that we believe are possible, power and responsibility must emanate from the school-building level. **Therefore, principals should be allowed some discretion in budgetary allocations that will permit flexibility in management.**

EDUCATING A PROFESSION

If the conditions of work were changed to support professional roles, if career ladders were established for restructuring teaching, and if compensation programs were reformed to provide competitive salaries and financial incentives for responsibility and high performance, there would remain the problem of how teachers should be educated, both in preservice preparation and continuing throughout their careers. In fact, the other changes would be empty without the strength of a well-qualified and appropriately educated and trained professional work force.

ISSUES OF QUALITY

Over the past decade, there has been a 53 percent decline in the number of graduates of teacher education programs. At the same time, the number of institutions offering such teacher education programs has increased by 10 percent, mostly in small private colleges.

Declines in teacher education enrollments are due mostly to declining student enrollment in the elementary and secondary schools. However, the National Center for Educational Statistics projects increasing enrollments over the next fifteen years. Such forecasts indicate a demand for 197,000 new teachers by 1986. Current teacher education enrollment and attrition patterns suggest that there will be only 160,000 new teachers available that year. That pattern is expected to prevail through the 1990s.

Increasing demand will expand supply in line with market forces. Classrooms will be filled and salaries will be driven up. However, the problem is how to recruit, develop, and retain *quality* teachers for the next two generations of American students.

A number of recent reports have provided important insights into the state of teacher education. A Carnegie Foundation study reported the following findings:[7]

■ Little data exist on teacher education students.

■ There is no uniformity in how teachers are educated.

■ Of the institutions with teacher education programs, 82 percent ignore Scholastic Aptitude Test and American College Test scores when considering teacher education applicants.

■ Only 47 percent of the institutions surveyed require passage of a competency test upon completion of the teacher education program.

■ The certification process varies enormously among states.

Perhaps the strongest indictment of teacher education comes from teachers themselves. In a survey of teacher attitudes, 50 percent of teachers polled felt their preparation did not serve them well in teaching. In fact, only 10 percent believed their training prepared them well for the classroom.[8]

In past years, teaching, although not well-compensated, was a high-status profession. Teachers enjoyed the respect of the students, parents, and the larger community. The low esteem in which teaching is now held can be solved in part by raising both standards and pay and by improving the quality of preparation programs. However, as we have already indicated, we believe that status is closely linked to teacher effectiveness. Making it difficult to become a teacher is not enough. What teachers learn in their professional education must better equip them to be effective in the classroom.

The recruitment, selection, and preparation of teachers are critical ingredients for improving the quality of teaching. Consistent with our view that improvement is contingent upon increasing the professionalism of teaching, we offer the following recommendations in the areas of standards, programs, and certification.

Standards. Standards for entrance into teacher education programs must be rigorous and highly selective, and graduation from a teacher education program should require the demonstration of competency in subject matter, professional knowledge, and professional skills.

There are now 1,240 institutions offering teacher education programs.

7. C. Emily Feistritzer, *The Conditions of Teaching* (Princeton: Carnegie Foundation for the Advancement of Teaching, 1983).

8. Metropolitan Life Insurance Company, Survey of the American Teacher, conducted by Louis Harris and Associates, Inc. (New York: Metropolitan Life Insurance Company, 1984).

Currently, teacher certification is directly tied to programs, and standards vary greatly from state to state. If teacher education programs are to become more rigorous and prestigious, they will have to compete for students on a national or regional basis. **Because we believe that uniformly high standards for teacher preparation programs can substantially upgrade the quality of new teachers, we recommend the establishment of a national commission on certification to address the issue of standards and how they might be satisfied.**

Programs. **We recommend that teacher candidates be required to complete a bachelor of arts or bachelor of sciences program with a major area of study other than education and to take the courses in education that will develop professional knowledge and professional skills.**

The classroom experience in a professional education program is central to the development of practical skills and socialization into the profession. Although there are excellent models for student teaching, this portion of the education program generally does not receive the attention it deserves. The use of outstanding practicing teachers as supervisors and mentors for student teachers is critical to the development of teacher skills and a positive professional self-image. Professors who are themselves excellent teachers are a necessary part of the teacher education process. Partnerships between universities and school districts that create clinical teaching professorships are one way of improving this process.

Another approach would be to shift the responsibility for strengthening the clinical training dimension of teacher education to the elementary and secondary schools themselves and make clinical training an internship and the first rung of the teaching career ladder. Responsibility for mentoring the novice teacher would fall to the master teachers in the school. Because the new teacher would be a part of the faculty, there would be greater incentive for the principal and staff to invest time and effort in his or her training and development. The training of new staff members could provide a vehicle for greater faculty interaction and problem solving. In addition, if the bulk of clinical training were transferred to a school-based postgraduation internship, it would free more time in the teacher education program for subject area courses.

However, additional training of new teachers would put a financial burden on school systems that few would be able to support. One solution to this problem could be state supplements to local school districts.

Certification. Meeting severe teacher shortages in certain subject areas will require strategies to attract some individuals who have the required training but who are not now teaching. Estimates are that there are now some 600,000 potential teachers in this category. **The certification process should be flexible enough to allow individuals attracted to teaching and qualified in a subject area to complete basic certification require-**

ments within a reasonable time period while on the job. One possibility is to hire these people as interns.

Encouraging mid-career shifts to teaching will require some incentive programs. The private sector might encourage this strategy by allowing employees early retirement without loss of benefits if they go into teaching. Portable retirement plans may be complicated but worth the trouble if they can encourage individuals to consider teaching at mid-career.

In-service training for working teachers represents another area of teacher education that has the potential for significant improvement. Currently, in most jurisdictions, salary schedules are keyed to taking a certain number of credits above the bachelor's degree, which may or may not lead to a masters or a doctorate. However, too often these courses are fragmented and unfocused and do not relate to a specific area of knowledge or improved classroom technique. **We recommend that coursework taken to satisfy requirements for salary increases should be more sharply focused and pertinent to teachers' professional knowledge and responsibilities.**

These recommendations do not represent the extent of reform that may be necessary to make teacher education the foundation for professional practice that it must become. However, they do represent the basic requirements for educating a profession, which we believe must be the framework for reform.

CONCLUSION:
THE FUTURE OF TEACHING

Recasting teaching into a respected, highly trained, and fairly compensated profession will require far-reaching changes in the structure and governance of the schools and the teaching profession. These changes imply an increasing shift of power down from the state, local, and administrative levels to the schools, where teachers and principals will assume distinctly different roles from those they now have—roles that are complementary rather than hierarchical.

Teachers will be increasingly responsible for the pedagogical decision making, curriculum planning, and instructional programs of the schools, both individually and on a collegial basis. Principals will provide organizational leadership and will retain control of organizational decision making. They will become the primary managers of schools, with budgetary authority and control over staffing decisions. The principals' authority will be guided by broad standards and goals agreed to by the local boards. Individual schools will grow into communities of shared interests with increasing decision-making authority, but they will be held accountable for a set of standards clearly established by the state and carried out by local boards.

Such changes put more control and decision-making authority at the school-building level, and should encourage and support the more active involvement of parents in the education of their children.

CHANGING ROLES FOR TEACHERS

In order for this restructuring to occur within the schools, there needs to be a major evolution in the roles of teachers, teacher organizations, and unions. Teacher unions have contributed enormously to improving the working conditions and salaries of the profession. However, it is also true that labor/management negotiations have contributed to adversarial roles that compound the difficulty of establishing community and consensus within the schools.

The time has come for teachers, administrators, and boards of education to recognize that such issues as the development of better evaluation systems, career ladders, entrance requirements, and a role for teachers in the governance of the profession and the schools represent a mutual agenda for change and improvement that extends beyond the collective bargaining process.

ROLES FOR THE BUSINESS COMMUNITY

We have illustrated throughout this report how the business community's experience with managing people is relevant to the problems of teacher quality and school effectiveness. **We recommend that links be created between schools and businesses for the purpose of transferring this understanding.**

For example, business can help school districts identify, select, and train principals as managers and organizational leaders. They can assist school systems in developing internal structures such as quality circles to support school-based decision making and increased professional roles.

Business people can work in the schools as tutors, aides, or advisors on curriculum-development teams. They can also train teachers in specific skills. Moreover, businesses can provide summer internships that offer valuable opportunities for teachers to work in a collegial environment in which their expectations for themselves and for working with others may be altered in important ways.

The business community can also bring its influence to bear at the policy level on behalf of reforms that will support the changes we believe are necessary for significant long-term improvement in the quality of teaching.

THE LONG VIEW

We do not expect that these changes will or can take place rapidly, easily, or by fiat. However, we do believe that major improvements in the quality of education depend upon improvements in the quality of teaching.

The atmosphere is right for education reform. We encourage legislatures, state boards of education, teacher-training institutions, local school boards, and the communities they represent to examine their policies and the recent proposals for reform to determine whether they are, in fact, contributing to or obstructing the development of greater professionalism in the teaching of our children.

CHAPTER 5

BUSINESS AND THE SCHOOLS: SHARED GOALS, COMMON INTERESTS

There is a legitimate role for the business community in the public schools. Business has much to gain from improvements in the quality of the schools, and it has a responsibility for helping to support and maintain that quality. Business also has a role to play in supporting adequate public funding for the schools.

American business has a long tradition of involvement in the public schools. Business leaders serve on school boards, and various industries are involved with vocational education. Businesses participate in cooperative education programs and provide student internships. Local small businesses often sponsor athletic and extracurricular activities.

However, much of this involvement with education has been on a case-by-case, project-by-project basis rather than as part of a systematic effort to make the most of business' resources.*

---

*See memorandum by DONALD E. GUINN (page 103).

GUIDELINES
FOR PRIVATE SECTOR
INVOLVEMENT

For business, several principles can be used to guide public-private interaction. In 1982, CED issued a major study of public-private partnerships in urban areas, and this study emphasized two such principles.[1] First, no business should engage in activities that run counter to the public interest, as defined through the political process. Second, public-private partnerships need to be defensible to stockholders, employees, and customers.

There is obviously a broad field for action within these guidelines. The decision to become actively involved in pursuing the goal of quality public education will be made by each business independently, but in each case it will be influenced by a number of factors. These will include the immediate needs of the school system and local traditions of collaborative involvement, internal cues such as the investment the company is making in remedial education and training and specific needs for trainable or technically educated employees, and the philosophical predisposition of the corporate culture and leadership.

INTERNAL FACTORS
AFFECTING INVOLVEMENT

Company size, corporate culture, growth, and wealth are all important considerations in the decision to become active in education. A small local business may need skilled, educated employees but may have few resources to direct toward involvement in schools. Frequently, small businesses use organizations such as the local chamber of commerce to leverage their commitments to local schools.

Large companies with greater resources have many options for involvement in education ranging from influencing national policy to working directly with school systems in plant locations. In addition, many corporations have a stated corporate policy on social involvement based on a sense of civic responsibility, self-interest, or both.

A company's wealth — technology, assets, and people — will also influence the decision. Companies in the service sector often see a direct benefit in educational involvement because they depend on the performance of people for productivity and profit. In contrast, some industrial

---

1. *Public-Private Partnerships: An Opportunity for Urban Communities* (New York: Committee for Economic Development, 1982), p. 92.

sectors are less dependent on human resources, and this may lead them to choose less direct ways to influence the quality of schools. In each case, however, the company needs to know what will be effective as well as what is appropriate.

Because the needs and conditions of public schools vary from one locale to another, the goal of business involvement will need to vary as well. **The company and the school system should determine together the appropriate goal of business involvement in a community.**

A company's readiness to deal with compromise and controversy will affect the decision about what a company might be willing to do to improve local schools. Its view of corporate public involvement will also be an important factor. Some companies see involvement in public education as a way of supporting employees' interests, and they seek direct benefits from these external activities.

The patterns of internal growth and reinvestment will affect a company's willingness to get involved. Small high technology firms, for example, may seem to have much to gain from improvements in education, but they are investing the least even though they depend greatly on skilled and educated employees.[2] Another factor driving these decisions may be the corporation's internal investments in education and training. Finally, growth or change in a corporation will affect both internal and external educational policy.

The company should ask these questions: How dependent is the economic life of the community on the school system? What are the precedents in the community for public-private cooperation? Which organizations or institutions can act as brokers or intermediaries between business and education? What public policies act as incentives or barriers? What alternatives exist for meeting the needs of the education system? What alternatives exist for meeting the educational needs of the business organization?

STRATEGIES FOR QUALITY PUBLIC SCHOOLS

Once a business has made the decision to become involved in education, it needs to take a broad, strategic look at what it wants to accomplish. Too often, businesses simply decide to "do something" for or about the public schools.* We see three basic strategies for corporate involvement:

---

2. Dale Mann, "All That Glitters: Public School/Private Sector Interaction in Twenty-Two U.S. Cities" (New York: Exxon Education Foundation, 1984); Elizabeth Ussem "Education and High Technology Industry: The Case of Silicon Valley," and "Education in a High Technology World: The Case of Route 128" (Boston: Northeastern University, Institute for the Interdisciplinary Study of Education, 1982).

---

*See memorandum by DONALD E. GUINN (page 104).

■ Supporting the existing system of education
■ Fostering innovative but incremental change
■ Working for major structural changes in the system

SUPPORTING THE EXISTING SYSTEM

Many school systems are basically sound, productive, and successful. They produce literate, competent individuals who pass the test for both employability and continuing education. Nevertheless, these systems may be experiencing problems such as falling enrollment, reduced funding, increasing demands for accountability, or sharply reduced public support. Businesses can help such schools by keeping laboratories and facilities up to date, aiding curriculum and staff development, and engendering support in the community.

Participation in programs such as career week at the local high school or sponsorship of scholarships can provide important benefits to students, teachers, and administrators. However, it implies acceptance of the existing goals and structures of the schools and is not the kind of action that leads to change and basic reform. Supporting the existing school system is an appropriate strategy for helping basically sound schools maintain quality education, but it will not be sufficient to turn a bad system around.

INNOVATIVE CHANGE, INCREMENTAL IMPROVEMENT

A middle-ground strategy for business involvement in public schools lies in finding and supporting creative opportunities for improvement that may or may not require structural change. Such activities may involve student development, teacher training, or improving the transition from school to work. Examples are projects that demonstrate the importance of teacher incentives and leadership development programs for school administrators. On the policy level, businesses can become involved in raising standards, increasing graduation requirements, and changing the length of the school day.

These projects constitute more creative responses to the needs of the schools. They stem from more strongly focused company decisions to become involved in education, and they raise important policy questions about the responsibilities and roles of the public and private sectors.

MAJOR STRUCTURAL REFORM

This strategy is based on the view that fundamental changes must be made in the public education system if it is to meet the goal of delivering quality education to our children. A business that adopts this strategy must deal with a number of complicated questions:

■ What is the appropriate role for the business community in motivating and implementing structural changes in public education?

■ What lessons has business learned about competition, organization, management, and leadership that are appropriate and transferable to public schools?

■ Can and should business use its influence to effect policy changes that would fundamentally alter the decision-making structure of public education at the state and local levels and in the school building?

We believe that the business community has an important role to play in achieving major structural reforms in education. The bottom-up strategy for school improvement developed in this policy statement is directed toward such basic reforms. If successfully carried out, this strategy could produce substantive improvements in the public schools. It is a strategy that is supported both by the experience of business and by its research on school effectiveness and effective teaching.

Many models and examples already exist for business involvement in fundamental reform. Although we strongly endorse increased business involvement in education, we also stress that businesses should approach involvement with public schools in the same way they approach any other major effort, by recognizing that the strategy for achieving a goal will differ with each locale depending on the needs, the environment, the businesses, and the school systems involved.

IMPLEMENTING THE STRATEGIES

Most corporate approaches to education take the form of financial support for specific activities, involvement in programs, policy change, or a combination of the three. However, any particular category of activity can serve more than one purpose. For example, program involvement can be designed to support an already sound system or it can foster major reform. Funding can support on-going programs or research that can lead to fundamental change (see figure, page 87).

PRIVATE-SECTOR FUNDING FOR PUBLIC EDUCATION

There are basically three major themes in the discussion of private-sector funding for public schools:

■ Could, should, or would the private sector finance the gap between the needs of the public schools and the public resources available to them?

■ How can private funds be used as "seed money" to extend or create opportunities for experimentation?

■ What is the role of business in funding projects or research and in developing initiatives that support improvements in public education?

We believe the business community cannot and should not be viewed as a significant source of funding for public education beyond its important role as a taxpayer in the community. Although corporations are currently giving between $12 and $15 million a year to public elementary and secondary education,[3] this is less than one-tenth of one percent of the total budget for elementary and secondary schools. The business sector's contribution in this area represents one-tenth of what the public schools are themselves raising from their own activities.

There are, however, many ways in which businesses can become directly involved in the funding of schools. In Cleveland, for example, the business community provided support for a media campaign that many credit for the passage of the first bond issue for the public schools in thirteen years. In other cities, members of the corporate community have accompanied superintendents to argue successfully before city and county councils for increased funding or to fend off significant budget cuts.

There is little doubt that the influence and power of the corporate community can be persuasive in arguing the case for renewed public financing of public schools. We believe this is an appropriate way in which the business community can lend its support.

PROJECT FUNDING

By funding special projects, business can provide a spirit of entrepreneurship and a willingness to experiment and take risks, which the public schools by themselves cannot achieve. In fact, project funding offers corporations and foundations an excellent opportunity to affect the instructional core of schooling: teaching and learning.

These activities do not need to be launched on a large scale to be effective. For example, Education Ventures, Inc., currently funded by seven Minnesota-based companies, has established the Teacher Venture Fund, which provided a total of $10,000 in grants in the 1984–85 school year in two districts in Minneapolis–St. Paul. The program will be expanded to include other districts in the future.

One noteworthy development has been the recent growth of community education funds and the establishment of the Public Education Fund (see page 88). These community-based funds provide, among other services, small grants to teachers to develop innovative classroom projects.

---

3. P. Michael Timpane, "Corporations and Public Education in the Cities" (New York: Carnegie Corporation, 1982), p. 38; Mann, "All that Glitters," p. 17.

TYPES OF PRIVATE-SECTOR INVOLVEMENT IN PUBLIC EDUCATION

Type of Involvement	STRATEGIES		
	System Support	Incremental Change	Structural Reform
Funding	Donation of Equipment	Public Education Funds Teacher Recognition Programs Minigrants Programs Public Relation Campaigns	Support of Major Research
Program Involvement	Career Days Speakers' Programs	Adopt-A-School Programs Management Training School-to-Work Programs Magnet School Development	
Policy Involvement	Local School Board Participation	State Education Task Forces	Major State Policy Initiatives ■ California Roundtable ■ Minnesota Business Partnership CED Statement on National Policy

Another program that makes use of small grants is IMPACT II, a program that promotes systemwide improvements in classroom instruction and professional interaction among teachers via the sharing of instructional innovations that individual teachers have developed in their classrooms. Minigrants are awarded both to teachers who have developed an innovation and teachers who wish to replicate the innovation. The Exxon Education Foundation funded the initial IMPACT II programs that were mounted

---

EDUCATION FUNDS
BUILDING COMMUNITY SUPPORT

A mechanism that has stimulated business and community involvement is the relatively recent development of hundreds of local education funds and foundations across the country. These funds (sometimes initially organized as an arm of a local school district and in other instances as a friendly, yet independent partner) have mobilized community leadership, raised limited amounts of private dollars for supportive programs, and have become third-party intermediaries for building new constituencies for a community's public schools.

In almost all instances, local business and corporate leadership are heavily represented on the boards of directors or advisory councils of these local education funds or foundations. Many have developed a strategy of targeting small grants in the form of limited private-sector contributions to teachers, principals, parent groups, and school districts for innovative projects. Awarding these minigrants has often served to improve school district morale, enhance the image of the school system, and increase the local leadership's understanding of, and involvement in, school issues.

On the basis of the successful experiences of the San Francisco Education Fund and the Allegheny Conference Education Fund in Pittsburgh, the Ford Foundation helped establish the Public Education Fund in 1983. This new national organization is providing technical and grant assistance to local education funds and foundations primarily in urban communities across the country. It will carry out a five-year program of assistance in more than forty cities and is launching a complementary effort in some smaller communities. The fund has also begun a rural initiative in cooperation with the Southern Education Foundation in the Southeast.

One issue that received early attention in the development of these local funds was the potential for inequity in school finance because some communities have a greater ability to generate private resources. Although there are several examples of this occurring in extremely affluent areas, initial expectations of large private-sector contributions to local education foundations have for the most part not been realized. In fact, in most urban communities, the local fund has served as a vehicle to equalize private support among district schools rather than as a supporter of those already gifted with a strong parent organization, alumni group, or corporate connections.

---

on a pilot basis in New York City and Houston. In addition, the foundation underwrote a three-year evaluation of the pilots. Since the pilot phase ended in late 1983, several school systems have begun similar programs, often with small seed-money grants from the Exxon Education Foundation.

Corporate dollars can also play a major role in education research and curriculum development and enrichment. For example, Atlantic Richfield has funded a major study of U.S. high schools, Standard Oil (Ohio) has made a major grant to the American Association for the Advancement of Science for curriculum development, and Phillips Petroleum has funded a number of films that have been widely used in the nation's classrooms.

The Council for Advancement of Private Higher Education uses foundation resources to leverage contributions made by major corporations to postsecondary institutions. A similar structure devoted to public elementary and secondary schools should be considered. **We believe there is a need for mechanisms to leverage corporate funds with money available from private foundations to broaden opportunities for public schools.** It is clear that corporate contributions can be increased from the current 5 percent of all corporate education giving and that the amount can be made to go further if adequately leveraged.

PROGRAM INVOLVEMENT

Program activities range from participation in local high school career weeks to systemwide adopt-a-school (or join-a-school) programs to complex partnerships between businesses and the schools. There can be benefits from all types of program involvement, but it is important that participants be realistic in their expectations and that they choose to be involved in activities which will meet their goals.

Adopting a school has become a highly visible form of business involvement, and this kind of relationship can cover a wide range of activities. Adopt-a-school programs may be districtwide or individually established. The company may be a large corporation (American Can Company, for example, has joined in a partnership with Martin Luther King, Jr., High School in New York City), a small business, a community organization, a nonprofit institution, or a church.

A recent survey by the U.S. Department of Education found that this kind of partnership was most likely to occur in large districts and central cities and that high schools were more frequently involved than elementary or junior high schools.[4] According to the survey, the most common kinds of support included guest speakers, demonstrations, donations of equipment, and special awards. However, only 7 percent of the districts responding to the Department of Education survey said that tutoring was done by corpo-

---

4. U.S. Department of Education, "Partnerships in Education: Education Trends of the Future," 1984.

rate volunteers, although this is an activity whose positive impact on students' reading and mathematics skills has been documented.[5]

Although most adopt-a-school programs are basically support efforts, they can play a significant role in engendering more general public support for the public schools. For example, the districtwide adopt-a-school program in Memphis, Tennessee, was specifically targeted to that goal. Following court-ordered desegregation, white enrollment in Memphis public schools dropped by 30,000, and public support for the schools was at an all-time low. The adopt-a-school program has not solved all of the problems of the Memphis schools, but it has stimulated greater business and community support and has increased white participation in the schools.

The Memphis experience highlights the fact that increased familiarity with the public schools can mitigate negative images and lead to wider and stronger support. Another benefit is that it helps to avoid the isolation from the larger community. Such programs can improve morale among students and faculty and can do the same for the business employees who become involved.

PUBLIC-PRIVATE PARTNERSHIPS

A more systematic, sustained interaction between business and the schools is the key characteristic of public-private partnerships. Partnerships are difficult to establish and maintain because they involve relationships between organizations and, to be effective, require the identification of shared and agreed-upon goals.

What is the spark that creates partnerships? Sometimes it is the scarcity or decline of available resources. Sometimes a crisis, such as court-ordered bussing, will spur collaborative action.

In organizing a partnership, it is important to remember that schools and businesses differ markedly in the ways in which people work and in which the work gets done. Schools are typically loosely coupled organizations with little coordination among working groups, whereas corporations are often tightly organized around technical production systems. There is often less emphasis on being a team player in the schools than in corporations.

Collaborative efforts involving school-based personnel must take these differences in style and expectations into account in order to avoid a collision between school and corporate cultures. This is often where partnership efforts break down.

Partnerships need to involve the school-based personnel; they also need to reach down into the employee ranks of the corporation if they are to have staying power and a positive impact. For businesses used to making

5. *Evaluation Study of School Volunteer Development Project*, Dade County, Florida, 1972–1975.

quick decisions, the slow, multilayered, bureaucratic process characteristic of many large school districts can make collaboration an arduous process.

The Honeywell Corporation's partnership experience with the Minneapolis public schools illustrates a successful effort that has kept these factors in mind. Both the school system and Honeywell entered into their collaboration only after a careful process of identifying the goals and strategies and the ways in which they could be carried out. Those shared by both the corporation and the school system were selected for targeted action.

Compatible goals and strategies are often not enough. To ensure proper communication, exchange, and feedback, *linking structures* may be needed. In some cases, these linking structures will have to be newly established. For example, the Committee to Support the Philadelphia Public Schools was formed to bring together university, business, foundation, and public school resources in a comprehensive effort to improve the Philadelphia public schools. The Committee to Support the Philadelphia Public Schools is an arm of the Greater Philadelphia First Corporation and its Urban Affairs Partnership. The committee includes chief executives of major companies, presidents of colleges and universities, and heads of two major foundations. Approximately seventy-five corporate executives, college and university personnel, and school administrators participate in subgroups focused on financial resources; teaching, learning, and curriculum; education for employment; and human resource management.

The Atlanta Partnership of Business and Education, Inc., is a nonprofit corporation whose members represent over 100 business and higher education institutions. Its purpose is to facilitate business-education partnerships with the public schools.

Some collaborative efforts have successfully utilized existing linking structures. For example, the Allegheny Conference, established in 1944 to help the corporate community in Pittsburgh carry out is civic agenda, has become a brokering agent for business, the school system, and citizens' groups. A great asset of the Allegheny Conference is that it has the long-standing confidence of both business and civic groups.

In most communities, businesses or business-related organizations provide the links, but both colleges and universities and some education associations also play either a direct or a supportive role. For example, a consortium of higher education institutions is active in Philadelphia, and the Boston Compact, described below, has been extended to universities and colleges in the area.

Intermediary or linking institutions can and do form partnerships and implement strategies that would not be possible for individual businesses acting independently. Participation in a state educational policy process is more likely to be successful if there is an intermediary, such as the California

Roundtable or the Minnesota Business Partnership. The kind of commitment made by companies in the Boston Compact to guarantee a specified number of jobs for graduating students who meet established academic performance standards would probably not be made by corporations acting alone. Some businesses may also prefer to work through intermediaries when controversial or high-risk projects are involved.

The importance of intermediary organizations should not obscure the key role often played by individuals in forming partnerships. Fundamentally, partnerships are created by *people*, not institutions. The strength, communication skills, perseverance, patience, and commitment of the individuals involved are the characteristics of success.

We urge businesses to examine the potential for improving education through existing intermediary organizations in the community and to take the lead in establishing new organizations if they are needed.

In successful partnerships, there is frequently an advocate or champion who is most visible and vigorous in seeing a collaborative project through from conception to implementation. To that we would add the importance of commitment from the top. Commitment from the chief executive officer of the corporation and from the superintendent in the school system is essential for a successful partnership. Only with that commitment will the appropriate resources and time be delegated to a collaborative effort.

However, this commitment from the top must reach deep into each organization to involve teachers and principals in school buildings and managers and workers in businesses. **Internalizing the partnership effort into the strategic operations of each organization must be done deliberately if the commitment is to have a life beyond the tenure of the individuals at the top**.

Different partnerships may have different objectives, but those reporting the highest success rates seem to share some basic characteristics:

- They have specific, mutually agreed-upon goals and objectives. Each partner knows what the other has to offer and has a realistic view of what might be accomplished.

- They are focused on the instructional core of schooling — students, teachers, and principals.

- They involve leveraging of both financial and human resources.

In addition, many successful partnership efforts seem to focus on one or more of the following specific objectives:

- Employability
- Curriculum and skill development
- Management and leadership

Employability. The business community has much to offer and much to gain from collaboration focused on employability. It has critical information to offer about what is required for successful employment and work sites for training, internships, and career development. Business also stands to benefit from a better-educated pool of potential employees and a better-educated public.

Business has traditionally had an active interest in programs to reduce high school dropout rates, provide work experience, and improve basic skills. But to date, there has been no systematic evaluation of these partnership programs to determine how successful they are in increasing employability. This kind of research needs to be done in order to identify the most effective private-sector strategies. The Philadelphia-based organization Public/Private Ventures is now conducting research on such programs involving disadvantaged youths.

Intermediary organizations, such as the Boston Private Industry Council (PIC), can often provide the most effective structure for pooling the available jobs of a large number of businesses in a particular city and providing a tangible link between job opportunities and measurable improvements in the school performance of disadvantaged, inner-city youth. The Boston PIC is performing this function as part of the Boston Compact, which is described in greater detail on page 94. The Compact is an agreement between the business community and the school system in Boston to give hiring priority to young people who have shown that they can meet higher attendance and academic standards in school. Founded in 1982, the Compact is currently providing over 600 permanent jobs to Boston high school graduates and 1,000 part-time and 2,000 summer jobs to students still in school.

Cooperative education is one of the oldest forms of partnership involving high schools and business. Employers provide paid work experience on job sites during the school year. Currently, approximately 500,000 high school students participate in some kind of cooperative education program.

The Philadelphia High School Academy Association, Inc. and the Murry Bergtraum High School in New York are two examples of successful cooperative education. The Philadelphia Academies are magnet programs focusing on electrical and electronic skills, automotive trades, business, and health. Each program provides work experience, stresses employability skills, and requires achievement in basic academic skills for graduation.

The Murry Bergtraum High School for Business Careers is a partnership between the New York public schools and the banking and finance community of lower Manhattan. Students at the school must not only fulfill the basic requirements for an academic diploma but must also complete a program in one of three areas in banking and finance. Dress, attendance, and performance requirements are modeled after those of the business commu-

THE BOSTON COMPACT
JOBS IN EXCHANGE FOR IMPROVED
SCHOOL PERFORMANCE

After nearly a decade of struggling to right the wrongs of segregation and the problems caused by a highly politicized school committee, the Boston Compact was created in 1982 as a way of linking improvements in school performance with job opportunities in Boston. Under the Compact, commitments were made to provide job opportunities and to improve school performance measurably in areas such as attendance, basic skills, and job and college preparation. The Boston PIC has helped organize available job opportunities, and in its first three years of existence, the Compact has spurred the following progress:

In the business community,

- 336 firms have signed the Compact "priority hiring" pledge;
- summer job hires have increased from 500 jobs in 1982 to 2,000 in 1985;
- over 600 graduates were hired in permanent jobs in the fall of 1984, and by March were earning an average of $5.35 an hour. Over 1,000 young people were working part-time under the Compact during the school year; and
- a career specialist, who works for the PIC and is paid with school department funds, is in nearly every high school, helping young people prepare for, find, and succeed in employment.

In the public schools,

- aggressive attendance outreach programs have raised average daily attendance in high schools from 77.7 percent in 1980–81 to 83.3 percent in 1983–84, and for juniors and seniors, the dropout rate has dipped slightly;
- high school reading scores are up five points since 1982–83 and mathematics scores are up eight points; and
- each high school has developed a strategy for using all available resources, including university and business assistance, to make progress toward the Compact goals.

In addition, twenty-five schools of higher education in the area have pledged to increase the admission of Boston public high school graduates by 25 percent over the next five years, and local trade unions have agreed to increase the number of public high school students accepted into apprenticeships each year by 5 percent.

nity. The curriculum was designed jointly with the business community, and upper-grade students participate in internship programs. The dropout rate is very low. Bergtraum graduates are in high demand upon graduation, but 85 percent of the students go on to postsecondary education.

Curriculum and Skill Development. Many companies aim their partnership efforts at developing specific skills and knowledge, and a major area of concern for both business and the schools is improving mathematical, scientific, and technological skills.

In the area of technology education, projects include donating equipment, computer training, and developing magnet school programs.

Some mathematics and science efforts are structured to work directly with students, sometimes with a special emphasis on the disadvantaged. The Peninsula Academies in the San Francisco Bay area and Project COFFEE (a partnership between Digital Equipment Corporation and the Oxford, Massachusetts, public schools) serve low-income students who are potential dropouts. Another program, the Philadelphia-based organization INROADS, seeks out talented minority high school seniors and college students to participate in a special program to help them prepare for careers in business, science, and engineering. Phillips Petroleum Company produces films on science and other topics that it circulates to schools on a free-loan basis. "The Search for Solutions" is a series of nine, eighteen-minute films that explore the process of scientific problem-solving. The film series is targeted to secondary students, particularly women and minorities, to encourage them to consider careers in science, engineering, and technology.

Several important programs focus on improving the teaching of science and mathematics. The GTE teacher-incentive program rewards outstanding science and mathematics teachers with grants for personal and professional development. GTE hopes such grants will help keep outstanding teachers in teaching. The Project to Increase the Mastery of Mathematics, a Wesleyan University program funded by the General Electric Foundation, described in greater detail on page 96, has launched a major effort to improve the teaching and learning of mathematics in the state's public schools.

Although science and technology are frequently the focus of partnerships, other noteworthy efforts are concerned with a broader range of skills. The Philadelphia Alliance for Teaching Humanities in the Schools (PATHS) is a partnership of business, higher education, and the Philadelphia School District. The first PATHS undertaking has been the Writing Project, designed to improve the teaching of writing throughout the curriculum. Other projects include minigrants for teachers, departments, and schools and a three-year curriculum-planning effort to be carried out by teachers, university professors, and administrators.

In New Hampshire, the Corporate Council for Critical Skills (CCCS) aims to improve the problem-solving abilities and critical-thinking skills of high school students. A consortium of some fifty New Hampshire businesses, CCCS runs training institutes for teachers in skills that can be applied throughout the curriculum. The program reports such a high level of teacher satisfaction, that two-thirds of the costs have now been assumed by the public sector. What is notable about both the PATHS and the CCCS programs is their focus on the teacher as the key to school improvement.

Many models exist for successful business involvement in skill and curriculum development. Interested businesses should strongly consider this area when exploring forms of private sector involvement in education.

Management and Leadership. One of the most useful contributions the business community can make is its expertise in management. This expertise should be available to schools in helping identify potential managers and training them for leadership roles.

In Minnesota, the St. Louis Park Schools and Honeywell have a partnership that includes training school administrators. The National Association of Secondary School Principals' Training Institutes were designed around corporate management training principles.

Business can also help in personnel and financial management. An eighty-five member task force of loaned executives from the business part-

---

THE GENERAL ELECTRIC FOUNDATION'S INCENTIVE PROGRAMS

Acting on the belief that motivated teachers create motivated students, the General Electric Foundation supports programs that provide both professional and community recognition of excellence in mathematics and science teaching.

■ **The Project to Increase the Mastery of Mathematics** provides support for "master" math teachers to attend an intensive summer institute at which they learn the latest teaching techniques and advancements in their field. Once the school year begins, these master teachers share their new findings with teachers in other schools.

■ **The Science Teacher Enrichment at Museums Program** helps teachers make use of resources such as science television shows, museum exhibits, local zoological associations, and botanical gardens. Teachers are also helped in developing classes for special groups in magnet schools and for gifted students.

■ **The Mini-Grants Program** awards up to $1,000 for innovative proposals submitted by teachers.

nership organization Chicago United has analyzed the Chicago schools' management, and the Los Angeles Chamber of Commerce has examined the Los Angeles schools' financial status. In Minneapolis, the corporate community has supported a long-term strategic planning process for the public schools. Numerous other school districts have formal and informal arrangements with the private sector that focus on improving school management, district operations, finance and budgeting, and material and facilities management (see below).

In addition to such arrangements, some school districts have been adapting management techniques from business and applying them to schools. The Muskegon, Michigan, school system has developed "quality interaction circles" using consensus decision-making processes to deal with a variety of school problems. Job fragmentation, a phenomenon in industry sometimes associated with poor-quality output, is also a problem in schools. Typically teachers are not involved in important decisions, such as textbook and test selection or curriculum development. Quality circles

---

FOCUS ON IMPROVING SCHOOL MANAGEMENT

The Council of the Great City Schools recently surveyed its member school districts to identify collaborative efforts with the private sector which are directed at improving school management, cost-effectiveness, and productivity. Some examples of these efforts include:

■ The Baltimore Ramsey Conference Group, whose members are business executives, makes recommendations for management strategies for the public schools.

■ The Atlanta public school system has long had a collaborative relationship with the local business community. Studies of school district management practices have been funded and conducted by personnel from Atlanta corporations, organized largely through the Chamber of Commerce.

■ In Dallas, the school system contracts with outside agencies and private-sector firms to assist with management needs. Personnel management, information systems, facilities utilization, and financial audits are the focus of such contractual arrangements.

■ In Dade County, Florida, the Dade Partners, representing local businesses, are involved in assisting the public schools with accounting procedures, training administrators, and providing specific consulting services.

SOURCE: Council of the Great City Schools, "A Survey and Analysis of School District/Private Sector/ University Cooperative Programs for Educational Improvement in the Great Cities." Unpublished paper prepared for the Ford Foundation, February 15, 1981.

may provide a way to ensure that teachers can be involved in such professional roles which are related to their efficiency in the classroom.

We strongly encourage more businesses to share their management expertise with the public schools.

POLITICS AND POLICY

Business-education partnerships at the school-building or district level have an enormous potential for improving the public schools. But increasingly, businesses are finding that political action at the state and local levels can bring important and broad-based improvements. Responsible corporate involvement at the political and policy levels can substantially broaden and strengthen the power base of the public schools.

Although business has traditionally been represented on local school boards, business participation at this level has dropped sharply in recent years. **We believe the business community needs to participate in the local policy-making process. Participation on local school boards by key managers should be encouraged and actively supported by their companies. Moreover, we urge business executives serving on local boards to give high priority to the bottom-up management strategies that we advocate in this report.**

In addition to school board participation, businesses in a number of communities have successfully supported their school systems in the political arena. In both Cleveland and Memphis, for example, business support helped win additional funding for the public schools.

At the state level, business has been heavily involved in numerous task forces established to address educational reform. In some states, business has led the reform movement. For example, business involvement in California and Minnesota demonstrates what can be accomplished by partnerships at the state level. In California, the business community became concerned about the decline in quality education after the passage of Proposition 13 in 1978. Rather than simply supporting increased taxes for funding the schools, the California Roundtable undertook a major study of state education programs in 1983, and on the basis of those findings, it worked extensively with the legislature and the governor to offer support from the business community for more money to education in exchange for a set of reforms designed to improve educational outcomes.

Concerned about a downward trend in Minnesota students' test scores, the Minnesota Business Partnership has recommended major structural reform for the schools, including institutionalizing mastery learning and a statewide voucher system for all eleventh and twelfth graders that would allow them to take advantage of alternative educational programs offered by industry, other high schools, and colleges and universities.

Neither these nor similar efforts are without critics, but they have demonstrated that the business community can affect policy decisions. We encourage businesses to work at both the local and the state levels to attain the goal of quality education.

In Chapter 2, we discussed the important leadership role that business can play in supporting the involvement of parents in the education of their children. Businesses can use in-house newsletters to provide information about schools and education issues. Employee networks can be used to encourage parents with shared interests to reach each other. Most important, corporations can develop flexible policies that encourage employees who are parents or who are otherwise interested to participate actively in their children's education and the community's schools. At least one company, Honeywell, is in the process of developing such a policy with its employees.

THE BUSINESS PERSPECTIVE

The business community has more than concern to offer in the quest for quality education. In program funding and policy, business has a perspective that is directly relevant to school improvement. The potential for business to become even more successfully involved in improving education is enormous. The recommendations contained in this statement have major policy and funding implications. We urge businesses individually and in association with others to participate actively in the forums in which these issues are discussed. Business has information about requirements for successful employment and experience and expertise about organization and management that can be invaluable.

Beyond the bottom-up management strategy for school improvement developed throughout this statement, we believe the business community's perspective on markets, competition, choice, utilization of research and development, and human resources can be applied successfully toward meeting the goals of the public schools. At the very least, we believe they should be tried in limited, controlled situations to learn how well they would work.

In addition to the business management practices described in Chapter 2, business can offer schools important expertise in two other areas: research and development and human resource development.

RESEARCH AND DEVELOPMENT

Business invests between 3 and 7 percent of sales dollars in research and development. That is an amount equivalent to roughly one-third of profits. Such a huge expenditure is justifiable because research and development activity is directly linked to improved productivity and profitability. It is the source of new and improved products and processes. By contrast, the federal research and development budget for elementary and secondary education is approximately $60 million; that is far less than 1 percent of total federal expenditures for elementary and secondary education.

To play a pivotal role in improving education, however, research and development must be not only well-planned and adequately funded, but also carefully attuned to the realities of the classroom. It needs champions, individuals who are devoted to linking the objectives of research and development to the needs of the practitioners and policy makers, and it needs systematic ways of ensuring that research has an impact on practice. Education has not made those links sufficiently or strongly enough and has therefore benefited much less than it could. (Specific recommendations on types of education research and development that warrant improvement are presented in Chapter 3.)

HUMAN RESOURCE DEVELOPMENT

Industry-based education and training represent a $40-billion investment directed at every level of employment and such diverse objectives as on-the-job skills training and education in the humanities for middle-level managers. Whatever the focus, this training is an investment in people that comes back to the organization in improved performance and commitment. In contrast, staff development in education is a low-funded, low-priority budget item for most school boards. It has traditionally been viewed as a pay increase for credits earned, with little or no attention paid to the specific needs of the individual or the school in which the teacher or administrator is employed. Although teaching is labor-intensive and highly interactive, and although schools are complex environments, very little attention is focused on building the skills of practitioners as individuals or on developing their commitment and ability to contribute to the school as an organization.

*   *   *

In order to make their efforts as fruitful as possible, both business and the schools must think strategically about what they do. In some cases, supporting and improving the existing structure is the best strategy for ensuring quality education. In others, comprehensive structural reform will be needed. The challenge for business and for the schools is to move forward together in pursuit of their shared goals and common interests.

MEMORANDA OF COMMENT, RESERVATION, OR DISSENT

Page 2, by ALFRED C. NEAL

My reservation with respect to our international competitiveness is that our trade deficits of recent years are attributable far less to deficiencies in education and the work ethic but more largely to an unprecedented over-valuation of the dollar that increased by more than 40 percent since 1980. The increase in imports has also grown from shifts of production, materials, and parts sources from U.S. to foreign sources with tractable labor, low wages, and often with minimum levels of education.

Page 4, by ROGER B. SMITH, with which ROY L. ASH has asked to be associated

I feel this report fails to deal adequately with many vital issues required to resolve the current debate on public education. First, the policy statement acknowledges that " . . . (public) schools, lacking competition, exhibit many of the characteristics of monopolies." However, the role of private education is ignored and a voucher system is rejected on the basis of possible damage to public schools even though no other real substitute is suggested. The report also emphasizes teacher salary increases without suggesting how higher teacher pay would mitigate a poor educational climate. Lack of student discipline and threats of violence have frustrated many teachers and caused more than a few to accept pay cuts in order to work in private schools. (See Toby Jackson, "Pay Isn't Foremost of Teacher Tribulations," *Wall Street Journal*, February 12, 1985, page 30.)

Page 4, by ROY L. ASH

A main conclusion expressed throughout this statement is that more money must be spent for public education. That may be right. But since we presume to offer a businesslike approach to the problems of education, it would be useful to make the reasoned case for that conclusion. In fact, just the opposite finding, i.e., ample money is even now being spent for public education, could be supported by the data in the report itself (pages 53 and 54) and other publicly available information.

Specifically, pages 53 and 54 data reveal, implicitly, that *non*-teacher expenditures rose, in constant dollars, 33 percent during the decade of the seventies. In current dollars, the non-teaching increase was from $21 billion in 1970 (of $41 billion spent in total) to $56 billion in 1980 (of $91 billion in total). All this was when public student enrollment was declining by 10 percent. Furthermore, public elementary and secondary school expenditures *per student*, expressed in constant dollars from a base of 100 in 1950, had increased to 160 by 1960, to 283 by 1970, and upward from there. Were the results commensurate?

A businesslike approach to education would fully explore and explain these significant cost growth trends, their causes and implications (especially any relating to the monopolistic nature of the public school system), and the possible internal savings opportunities that might be made before adopting the conclusion, by assertion only, that even more public funds are needed.

Pages 6 and 15, by FRANKLIN A. LINDSAY

The policy statement is excellent and I fully support the recommendations. However, I am concerned that in our emphasis on teaching basic skills, on problem-solving ability, and on adaptability to change, the importance of fostering creativity has been overlooked. A decade or two ago creativity was overemphasized to the detriment of the basics. But we should not now fall into the trap of over correcting past mistakes.

Pages 9 and 23, by DONALD E. GUINN, with which ROY L. ASH and ROCCO C. SICILIANO have asked to be associated

Every child should be given the opportunity to reach his/her full potential. As such, the gifted and talented should not be forgotten from an education reform perspective. Technological change and global competition call for creative thinkers, superior talent, and wise leaders in every sector of the economy. America's gifted and talented represent the next generation of leaders in our society. It is a fallacy that bright kids can make it on their own. Many of these children are bored by the slow pace of the average class and become dropouts. Many never reach college. Only 20 percent of the teachers in gifted education are properly trained to design curriculum for these students. Additionally, gifted education is not readily available through regular school programs due to funding constraints. There are an estimated 2.5 million elementary and secondary students that fall within the category as defined by the Gifted and Talented Children's Education Act of 1978.

Page 17, by THOMAS J. EYERMAN

I would like to emphasize that, as noted here, education is not so much a knowledge that can be taught but what is perceived by the student. The concepts of striving for excellence, priority setting, and human relations are not to be learned from a textbook but from the example of the parent, teacher, and the environment in which the textbook education is given.

A school that has all of the most up-to-date facilities may not be the message that should be communicated to the student. We must be concerned with both the intellectual as well as physical environments in which the invisible curriculum is taught in conjunction with the textbook education.

Page 22, by THOMAS J. EYERMAN

The extracurricular activities such as athletics, music, etc. are where the invisible curriculum is taught by example of the other students and the faculty. This is where the concept of human relations can be expressed and a student taught by example of interpersonal relationships.

Page 69, by ROBERT W. LUNDEEN

We pass too easily over the added responsibilities which have been laid on the classroom teacher because of the economic and social changes which have led to declining parental control and involvement. With the larger numbers of two working parents and single-parent families, the teacher may well be the only counselor and role model available for many students. To help assure equity along with excellence in our public education system, business leaders in each community should specifically address the needs of the classroom teacher for increased compensation and added time to assume this vital "proxy parent" role in value building and character development.

Page 81, by DONALD E. GUINN

It would be extremely useful if CED's report included an appendix of the names, addresses, and telephone numbers for the many programs mentioned in the report, so that business staff persons can obtain additional information on individual projects.

Page 83, by DONALD E. GUINN

The California Chamber Education Committee publication *A Sure Bet: Business and Education Together — A Handbook for Chamber of Commerce Education Committees* provides a step by step guide to establishing and guiding community partnerships in support of local education.

The California Roundtable developed a comprehensive publication *A Catalog of Business and Community Programs*. The catalog demonstrates the present range of business and community partnerships in support of local education in California. More than 600 programs in twenty-three categories are described in the catalog. It can be used by businesses, schools, and community groups who would like to join or establish similar programs.

We wish to give special thanks to the following foundations and companies whose generous support made this policy statement possible.

J. Howard Pew Freedom Trust

Metropolitan Life Foundation

The Edna McConnell Clark Foundation

Exxon Education Foundation

The Ford Foundation

The Procter & Gamble Fund

R. J. Reynolds Industries, Inc.

John M. Olin Foundation, Inc.

The William & Flora Hewlett Foundation

Atlantic Richfield Foundation

Federated Department Stores, Inc. Foundation

Northrop Corporation

The Pfizer Foundation, Inc.

The Standard Oil Company (Ohio)

Phillips Petroleum Foundation, Inc.

Hospital Corporation of America

Following is a list of the research papers prepared as background for the CED Subcommittee on Business and the Schools. These papers will be published by CED in a separate volume.

Employers and High Schools: The Fit Between Learning and Working
Paul E. Barton, assessment policy committee liaison, National Assessment of Educational Progress, Educational Testing Service

American Business and Public Education: The Question of Quality
Denis P. Doyle, resident fellow in education, American Enterprise Institute for Public Policy Research, and Marsha Levine, education consultant, American Enterprise Institute for Public Policy Research

Vocational Education in America
E. Gareth Hoachlander, MPR Associates, Inc.

The California Roundtable: Their Strategy and Impact on State Education Policy
Michael W. Kirst, professor of education, Stanford University

A Consumer's Guide to a National Census of Educational Quality
Barbara Lerner, Lerner & Associates

Summary of Report: Survey of Employer Needs
School Reform: A Role for the American Business Community
Excellence in Education: Lessons from America's Best-Run Companies and Schools
Marsha Levine

Education and the Private Sector
Marsha Levine and Denis P. Doyle

Financing Education Excellence
Allan Odden, associate professor, University of Southern California

A Legacy for the 21st Century: Investment Opportunities in Our Children's Schooling
Daniel H. Saks, professor of education policy and of economics, Institute for Public Policy Studies, Vanderbilt University

Vocational Education: The Missing Link?
Nathaniel M. Semple, vice president and director of governmental affairs, Committee for Economic Development

Teacher Compensation: The Need for a New Direction
William H. Wilken, associate professor of education, George Mason University

OBJECTIVES OF THE COMMITTEE FOR ECONOMIC DEVELOPMENT

For over forty years, the Committee for Economic Development has been a respected influence on the formation of business and public policy. CED is devoted to these two objectives:

To develop, through objective research and informed discussion, findings and recommendations for private and public policy that will contribute to preserving and strengthening our free society, achieving steady economic growth at high employment and reasonably stable prices, increasing productivity and living standards, providing greater and more equal opportunity for every citizen, and improving the quality of life for all.

To bring about increasing understanding by present and future leaders in business, government, and education, and among concerned citizens, of the importance of these objectives and the ways in which they can be achieved.

CED's work is supported strictly by private voluntary contributions from business and industry, foundations, and individuals. It is independent, nonprofit, nonpartisan, and nonpolitical.

The two hundred trustees, who generally are presidents or board chairmen of corporations and presidents of universities, are chosen for their individual capacities rather than as representatives of any particular interests. By working with scholars, they unite business judgment and experience with scholarship in analyzing the issues and developing recommendations to resolve the economic problems that constantly arise in a dynamic and democratic society.

Through this business-academic partnership, CED endeavors to develop policy statements and other research materials that commend themselves as guides to public and business policy; that can be used as texts in college economics and political science courses and in management training courses; that will be considered and discussed by newspaper and magazine editors, columnists, and commentators; and that are distributed abroad to promote better understanding of the American economic system.

CED believes that by enabling businessmen to demonstrate constructively their concern for the general welfare, it is helping business to earn and maintain the national and community respect essential to the successful functioning of the free enterprise capitalist system.

CED BOARD OF TRUSTEES

Chairman
EDMUND B. FITZGERALD, Chairman and Chief
   Executive Officer
Northern Telecom Limited

Vice Chairmen
OWEN B. BUTLER, Chairman of the Board
The Procter & Gamble Company

WILLIAM S. EDGERLY, Chairman of the Board and
   President
State Street Bank and Trust Company

PHILIP M. HAWLEY, Chairman of the Board
Carter Hawley Hale Stores, Inc.

JAMES L. KETELSEN, Chairman and Chief Executive
   Officer
Tenneco Inc.

FRANKLIN A. LINDSAY, Chairman
Engenics, Inc.

Treasurer
JOHN B. CAVE, Executive Vice President—
   Finance
McGraw-Hill, Inc.

EDWARD L. ADDISON, President
The Southern Company

HOWARD P. ALLEN, Chairman and Chief Executive
   Officer
Southern California Edison Company

ROY L. ASH
Los Angeles, California

H. B. ATWATER, JR., Chairman of the Board and Chief
   Executive Officer
General Mills, Inc.

RALPH E. BAILEY, Chairman and Chief Executive
   Officer
Conoco Inc.

ROBERT H. B. BALDWIN, Chairman, Advisory Board
Morgan Stanley & Co. Incorporated

NORMAN BARKER, JR., Chairman of the Board
First Interstate Bank of California

J. DAVID BARNES, Chairman and Chief Executive
   Officer
Mellon Bank N.A.

Z. E. BARNES, Chairman and Chief Executive Officer
Southwestern Bell Corporation

WARREN L. BATTS, President
Dart & Kraft, Inc.

ROBERT A. BECK, Chairman and Chief Executive
   Officer
The Prudential Insurance Company of America

PHILIP E. BEEKMAN, President
Joseph E. Seagram & Sons, Inc.

JACK F. BENNETT, Senior Vice President
Exxon Corporation

JAMES F. BERÉ, Chairman and Chief Executive Officer
Borg-Warner Corporation

DEREK C. BOK, President
Harvard University

JOAN T. BOK, Chairman
New England Electric System

THOMAS E. BOLGER, Chairman of the Board and
   Chief Executive Officer
Bell Atlantic Corporation

ALAN S. BOYD, Chairman
Airbus Industrie of North America

WILLIAM H. BRICKER, Chairman and Chief Executive
   Officer
Diamond Shamrock Corporation

ANDREW F. BRIMMER, President
Brimmer & Company, Inc.

ALFRED BRITTAIN III, Chairman of the Board
Bankers Trust Company

PERRY G. BRITTAIN, Chairman of the Board and
   Chief Executive Officer
Texas Utilities Company

CEES BRUYNES, Chairman, President and Chief
   Executive Officer
North American Philips Corporation

JOHN H. BRYAN, JR., Chairman and Chief Executive
   Officer
Sara Lee Corporation

THEODORE A. BURTIS, Chairman of the Board
Sun Company, Inc.

OWEN B. BUTLER, Chairman of the Board
The Procter & Gamble Company

*FLETCHER L. BYROM, Retired Chairman
Koppers Company, Inc.

ROBERT J. CARLSON, Chairman, President and Chief
   Executive Officer
BMC Industries Inc.

RAFAEL CARRION, JR., Chairman of the Board
Banco Popular de Puerto Rico

R. E. CARTLEDGE, President
Union Camp Corporation

JOHN B. CAVE, Executive Vice President—
   Finance
McGraw-Hill, Inc.

HUGH M. CHAPMAN, Chairman of the Board
Citizens & Southern National Bank of South Carolina

ROBERT A. CHARPIE, President
Cabot Corporation

ROBERT CIZIK, Chairman and President
Cooper Industries, Inc.

DAVID R. CLARE, President
Johnson & Johnson

DONALD C. CLARK, Chairman of the Board and Chief
   Executive Officer
Household International

ROBERT B. CLAYTOR, Chairman and Chief Executive
   Officer
Norfolk Southern Corporation

W. GRAHAM CLAYTOR, JR., Chairman and President
Amtrak

*Life Trustee

JOHN L. CLENDENIN, Chairman of the Board
BellSouth Corporation

*EMILIO G. COLLADO, Executive Chairman
International Planning Corporation

DOUGLAS D. DANFORTH, Chairman
Westinghouse Electric Corporation

D. RONALD DANIEL, Managing Director
McKinsey & Company, Inc.

RONALD R. DAVENPORT, Chairman of the Board
Sheridan Broadcasting Corporation

RALPH P. DAVIDSON, Chairman of the Board
Time Inc.

BARBARA K. DEBS, Corporate Director
Greenwich, Connecticut

ALFRED C. DeCRANE, JR., President
Texaco Inc.

ROBERT F. DEE, Chairman of the Board
SmithKline Beckman Corporation

ROBERT A. dePALMA, Senior Vice President and Chief
Financial Officer
Rockwell International Corporation

WILLIAM N. DERAMUS III, Chairman
Kansas City Southern Industries, Inc.

PETER A. DEROW, President
CBS/Publishing Group

JOHN DIEBOLD, Chairman
The Diebold Group, Inc.

GEORGE C. DILLON, Chairman of the Board
Butler Manufacturing Company

ROBERT R. DOCKSON, Chairman of the Board and
Chief Executive Officer
California Federal Savings and Loan Association

EDWIN D. DODD, Chairman Emeritus
Owens-Illinois, Inc.

DONALD J. DONAHUE, Retired Chairman
KMI Continental Inc.

JOHN T. DORRANCE, JR., Chairman of the Executive
Committee
Campbell Soup Company

JOSEPH P. DOWNER, Vice Chairman of the Board
Atlantic Richfield Company

FRANK P. DOYLE, Senior Vice President
General Electric Company

VIRGINIA A. DWYER, Senior Vice President—Finance
AT&T

W. D. EBERLE, President
Manchester Associates, Ltd.

WILLIAM S. EDGERLY, Chairman of the Board and
President
State Street Bank and Trust Company

JOHN R. EDMAN, Vice President
General Motors Corporation

JOHN C. EMERY, JR., Chairman, President and Chief
Executive Officer
Emery Air Freight Corporation

ROBERT F. ERBURU, President
The Times Mirror Company

WILLIAM T. ESREY, President and Chief Executive
Officer
United Telecommunications, Inc.

J. LEE EVERETT III, Chairman and Chief Executive
Officer
Philadelphia Electric Company

LYLE EVERINGHAM, Chairman of the Board and Chief
Executive Officer
The Kroger Co.

THOMAS J. EYERMAN, Partner
Skidmore, Owings & Merrill

JAMES B. FARLEY, Senior Chairman
Booz·Allen & Hamilton Inc.

DAVID C. FARRELL, President and Chief Executive
Officer
The May Department Stores Company

JOHN H. FILER, Former Chairman
Aetna Life and Casualty Company

EDMUND B. FITZGERALD, Chairman and Chief
Executive Officer
Northern Telecom Limited

JOSEPH B. FLAVIN, Chairman and Chief Executive
Officer
The Singer Company

*WILLIAM H. FRANKLIN, Chairman of the Board, Retired
Caterpillar Tractor Co.

ROBERT E. FRAZER, Chairman
The Dayton Power and Light Company

ROBERT R. FREDERICK, President and Chief Executive
Officer
RCA Corporation

HARRY L. FREEMAN, Executive Vice President,
Corporate Affairs and Communications
American Express Company

THOMAS F. FRIST, JR., M.D., President and Chief
Executive Officer
Hospital Corporation of America

ROBERT F. FROEHLKE, Chairman of the Board
Equitable Life Assurance Society of the United States

GERALD W. FRONTERHOUSE, President and Chief
Executive Officer
RepublicBank Corporation

H. LAURANCE FULLER, President
Amoco Corporation

DONALD E. GARRETSON, Community Service
Executive Program
3M Company

CLIFTON C. GARVIN, JR., Chairman of the Board
Exxon Corporation

RICHARD L. GELB, Chairman
Bristol-Myers Company

WALTER B. GERKEN, Chairman of the Board
Pacific Mutual Life Insurance Company

PIERRE GOUSSELAND, Chairman of the Board and
Chief Executive Officer
AMAX Inc.

THOMAS C. GRAHAM, Vice Chairman and Chief
Operating Officer—Steel & Related Resources
United States Steel Corporation

EARL G. GRAVES, President
Earl G. Graves Ltd.

HARRY J. GRAY, Chairman and Chief Executive Officer
United Technologies Corporation

W. GRANT GREGORY, Chairman of the Board
Touche Ross & Co.

DAVID L. GROVE, President
David L. Grove, Ltd.

DONALD E. GUINN, Chairman and Chief Executive
Officer
Pacific Telesis Group

JOHN H. GUTFREUND, Chairman and Chief Executive
Officer
Phibro-Salomon Inc.

RICHARD P. HAMILTON, Chairman, President, and
Chief Executive Officer
Hartmarx Corp.

RICHARD W. HANSELMAN, Chairman, President and
    Chief Executive Officer
Genesco Inc.

ROBERT A. HANSON, Chairman and Chief Executive
    Officer
Deere & Company

PAUL HARDIN, President
Drew University

CHARLES M. HARPER, Chairman of the Board and
    Chief Executive Officer
ConAgra, Inc.

FRED L. HARTLEY, Chairman and President
Unocal Corporation

BARBARA B. HAUPTFUHRER, Corporate Director
Huntingdon Valley, Pennsylvania

ARTHUR HAUSPURG, Chairman of the Board
Consolidated Edison Company of New York, Inc.

PHILIP M. HAWLEY, Chairman of the Board
Carter Hawley Hale Stores, Inc.

RAYMOND A. HAY, Chairman of the Board and Chief
    Executive Officer
The LTV Corporation

HAROLD W. HAYNES, Executive Vice President
    and Chief Financial Officer
The Boeing Company

RALPH L. HENNEBACH, Chairman
ASARCO Incorporated

LAWRENCE HICKEY, Chairman
Stein Roe & Farnham

RODERICK M. HILLS, Of Counsel
Latham, Watkins & Hills

ROBERT C. HOLLAND, President
Committee for Economic Development

LEON C. HOLT, JR., Vice Chairman and Chief
    Administrative Officer
Air Products and Chemicals, Inc.

ROY M. HUFFINGTON, Chairman of the Board
Roy M. Huffington, Inc.

WILLIAM S. KANAGA, Chairman
Arthur Young

DAVID T. KEARNS, Chairman & Chief Executive Officer
Xerox Corporation

GEORGE M. KELLER, Chairman of the Board
Chevron Corporation

DONALD P. KELLY, President
Kelly Briggs & Associates, Inc.

JAMES M. KEMPER, JR., Chairman of the Board
Commerce Bancshares, Inc.

J. C. KENEFICK, Chairman
Union Pacific System

JAMES L. KETELSEN, Chairman and Chief Executive
    Officer
Tenneco Inc.

TOM KILLEFER, Chairman Emeritus
United States Trust Company of New York

CHARLES M. KITTRELL, Executive Vice President
Phillips Petroleum Company

PHILIP M. KLUTZNICK, Senior Partner
Klutznick Investments

CHARLES F. KNIGHT, Chairman and Chief Executive
    Officer
Emerson Electric Co.

RALPH LAZARUS, Chairman, Executive Committee
Federated Department Stores, Inc.

DREW LEWIS, Chairman and Chief Executive Officer
Warner Amex Cable Communications

FLOYD W. LEWIS, Chairman and President
Middle South Utilities, Inc.

FRANKLIN A. LINDSAY, Chairman
Engenics, Inc.

HOWARD M. LOVE, Chairman and Chief Executive
    Officer
National Intergroup, Inc.

FRANCIS P. LUCIER, Chairman and Chief Executive
    Officer
Mohawk Data Sciences Corporation

ROBERT W. LUNDEEN, Chairman of the Board
The Dow Chemical Company

JACK A. MacALLISTER, President and Chief Executive
    Officer
U S WEST, Inc.

BRUCE K. MacLAURY, President
The Brookings Institution

WILLIAM A. MARQUARD, Chairman and Chairman,
    Executive Committee
American Standard Inc.

WILLIAM F. MAY, President
Statue of Liberty — Ellis Island Foundation, Inc.

ALONZO L. McDONALD, Chairman and Chief
    Executive Officer
Avenir Group, Inc.

JOHN F. McGILLICUDDY, Chairman of the Board and
    Chief Executive Officer
Manufacturers Hanover Corporation

JAMES W. McKEE, JR., Chairman
CPC International Inc.

JOHN A. McKINNEY, Chairman of the Board and Chief
    Executive Officer
Manville Corporation

CHAMPNEY A. McNAIR, Vice Chairman
Trust Company of Georgia

ROBERT E. MERCER, Chairman of the Board
The Goodyear Tire & Rubber Company

RUBEN F. METTLER, Chairman of the Board and Chief
    Executive Officer
TRW Inc.

RONALD T. MILLER, Chairman
Northwest Natural Gas Company

GEORGE F. MOODY, President and Chief Executive
    Officer
Security Pacific National Bank

STEVEN MULLER, President
The Johns Hopkins University

JOSEPH NEUBAUER, Chairman, President and Chief
    Executive Officer
ARA Services, Inc.

BARBARA W. NEWELL, Chancellor
State University System of Florida

EDWARD N. NEY, Chairman of the Board
Young & Rubicam Inc.

JAMES J. O'CONNOR, Chairman and President
Commonwealth Edison Company

WILLIAM S. OGDEN, Chairman and Chief Executive
    Officer
Continental Illinois National Bank and Trust
    Company of Chicago

LEIF H. OLSEN, Economic Consultant
Citibank, N.A.

JOHN D. ONG, Chairman of the Board
The BFGoodrich Company

*Life Trustee

ANTHONY J. F. O'REILLY, President and Chief
   Executive Officer
H. J. Heinz Company

NORMA PACE, Senior Vice President
American Paper Institute

VICTOR H. PALMIERI, Chairman
Victor Palmieri and Company Incorporated

DANIEL PARKER, Honorary Chairman
The Parker Pen Company

CHARLES W. PARRY, Chairman and Chief Executive
   Officer
Aluminum Company of America

PETER G. PETERSON, Chairman
Peterson, Jacobs & Company

JOHN J. PHELAN, JR., Chairman and Chief Executive
   Officer
New York Stock Exchange, Inc.

DEAN P. PHYPERS, Senior Vice President
IBM Corporation

HAROLD A. POLING, President
Ford Motor Company

EDMUND T. PRATT, JR., Chairman of the Board
Pfizer Inc.

LELAND S. PRUSSIA, Chairman of the Board
Bank of America N.T. & S.A.

JOHN R. PURCELL, Chairman and President
SFN Companies, Inc.

ALLAN L. RAYFIELD, President and Chief Operating
   Officer—Diversified Products and Services Group
GTE Service Corporation

FRANK H. T. RHODES, President
Cornell University

JAMES Q. RIORDAN, Senior Vice President
Mobil Corporation

S. DONLEY RITCHEY, Chairman
Lucky Stores, Inc.

BURNELL R. ROBERTS, Chairman and Chief Executive
   Officer
The Mead Corporation

KENNETH L. ROBERTS, Chairman and Chief Executive
   Officer
First American Corporation

BRUCE M. ROCKWELL, Chairman of the Board
Colorado National Bank

IAN M. ROLLAND, Chairman
Lincoln National Life Insurance Company

FRANCIS C. ROONEY, JR., Chairman of the Board
Melville Corporation

DONALD K. ROSS, Chairman of the Board
New York Life Insurance Company

THOMAS F. RUSSELL, Chairman and Chief Executive
   Officer
Federal-Mogul Corporation

JOHN SAGAN, Vice President—Treasurer
Ford Motor Company

RALPH S. SAUL, Former Chairman
CIGNA Corporation

HENRY B. SCHACHT, Chairman of the Board and Chief
   Executive Officer
Cummins Engine Company, Inc.

ROBERT M. SCHAEBERLE, Chairman
Nabisco Brands Inc.

GEORGE A. SCHAEFER, Chairman and Chief Executive
   Officer
Caterpillar Tractor Co.

WILLIAM A. SCHREYER, Chairman, President and
   Chief Executive Officer
Merrill Lynch & Co. Inc.

DONALD J. SCHUENKE, President and Chief Executive
   Officer
Northwestern Mutual Life Insurance Company

ROBERT G. SCHWARTZ, Chairman of the Board
Metropolitan Life Insurance Company

J. L. SCOTT, Chairman and Chief Executive Officer
J. L. Scott Enterprises, Inc.

S. F. SEGNAR, Chairman, President and Chief Executive
   Officer
InterNorth, Inc.

DONNA E. SHALALA, President
Hunter College

MARK SHEPHERD, JR., Chairman
Texas Instruments Incorporated

WALTER V. SHIPLEY, Chairman and Chief Executive
   Officer
Chemical Bank

ROCCO C. SICILIANO, Chairman, Executive
   Committee
Ticor

ANDREW C. SIGLER, Chairman and Chief Executive
   Officer
Champion International Corporation

RICHARD D. SIMMONS, President
The Washington Post Company

L. EDWIN SMART, Chairman of the Board
Transworld Corporation

FREDERICK W. SMITH, Chairman and Chief Executive
   Officer
Federal Express Corporation

PHILIP L. SMITH, President and Chief Operating
   Officer
General Foods Corporation

RICHARD M. SMITH, Vice Chairman
Bethlehem Steel Corporation

ROGER B. SMITH, Chairman
General Motors Corporation

SHERWOOD H. SMITH, JR., Chairman and President
Carolina Power & Light Company

ELMER B. STAATS, Former Comptroller General of the
   United States
Washington, D.C.

DELBERT C. STALEY, Chairman and Chief Executive
   Officer
NYNEX Corporation

DONALD M. STEWART, President
Spelman College

WILLIAM P. STIRITZ, Chairman of the Board
Ralston Purina Company

*WILLIAM C. STOLK
Easton, Connecticut

ELLEN S. STRAUS, President and General Manager
WMCA Radio

BARRY F. SULLIVAN, Chairman of the Board
First National Bank of Chicago

HOWARD R. SWEARER, President
Brown University

MORRIS TANENBAUM, Executive Vice President
AT&T

G. J. TANKERSLEY, Chairman
Consolidated Natural Gas Company

DAVID S. TAPPAN, JR., Chairman and Chief Executive
   Officer
Fluor Corporation

EDWARD R. TELLING, Chairman of the Board
Sears, Roebuck and Co.

ANTHONY P. TERRACCIANO, Vice Chairman, Global
   Banking
The Chase Manhattan Bank, N.A.

WALTER N. THAYER, Chairman
Whitney Communications Company

W. BRUCE THOMAS, Vice Chairman of
   Administration and Chief Financial Officer
United States Steel Corporation

L. S. TURNER, JR.
Dallas, Texas

THOMAS V. H. VAIL, President, Publisher and Editor
Plain Dealer Publishing Company

THOMAS A. VANDERSLICE, President and Chief
   Executive Officer
Apollo Computer Inc.

HANS W. WANDERS, President
The Wachovia Corporation

ALVA O. WAY, Chairman, Finance Committee
The Travelers Corporation

ARNOLD R. WEBER, President
Northwestern University

SIDNEY J. WEINBERG, JR., Partner
Goldman, Sachs & Co.

WILLIAM L. WEISS, Chairman of the Board
Ameritech

JOHN F. WELCH, JR., Chairman of the Board
General Electric Company

CLIFTON R. WHARTON, JR., Chancellor
State University of New York

ALTON W. WHITEHOUSE, JR., Chairman
The Standard Oil Company (Ohio)

HAROLD M. WILLIAMS, President
The J. Paul Getty Trust

J. KELLEY WILLIAMS, President
First Mississippi Corporation

JOSEPH D. WILLIAMS, Chairman of the Board and
   Chief Executive Officer
Warner-Lambert Company

THOMAS R. WILLIAMS, Chairman and President
First Atlanta Corporation

*W. WALTER WILLIAMS
Seattle, Washington

J. TYLEE WILSON, Chairman and Chief Executive
   Officer
R. J. Reynolds Industries, Inc.

MARGARET S. WILSON, Chairman of the Board
Scarbroughs

RICHARD D. WOOD, Chairman of the Board
Eli Lilly and Company

WILLIAM S. WOODSIDE, Chairman
American Can Company

M. CABELL WOODWARD, JR., Executive Vice
   President and Chief Financial Officer
ITT Corporation

CHARLES J. ZWICK, Chairman and Chief Executive
   Officer
Southeast Banking Corporation

*Life Trustee

HONORARY TRUSTEES

RAY C. ADAM, Retired Chairman
NL Industries, Inc.

E. SHERMAN ADAMS
New Preston, Connecticut

CARL E. ALLEN
North Muskegon, Michigan

JAMES L. ALLEN, Honorary Chairman
Booz·Allen & Hamilton Inc.

O. KELLEY ANDERSON
Boston, Massachusetts

ROBERT O. ANDERSON, Chairman of the
    Board
Atlantic Richfield Company

SANFORD S. ATWOOD
Lake Toxaway, North Carolina

JOSEPH W. BARR, Corporate Director
Arlington, Virginia

HARRY HOOD BASSETT, Chairman, Executive
    Committee
Southeast Bank N.A.

S. CLARK BEISE, President (Retired)
Bank of America N.T. & S.A.

GEORGE F. BENNETT, President
State Street Research & Management Company

HAROLD H. BENNETT
Salt Lake City, Utah

HOWARD W. BLAUVELT
Charlottesville, Virginia

JOSEPH L. BLOCK, Former Chairman
Inland Steel Company

ROGER M. BLOUGH
Hawley, Pennsylvania

FRED J. BORCH
New Canaan, Connecticut

MARVIN BOWER, Director
McKinsey & Company, Inc.

R. MANNING BROWN, JR., Director
New York Life Insurance Co., Inc.

JOHN L. BURNS, President
John L. Burns and Company

THOMAS D. CABOT, Honorary Chairman of the
    Board
Cabot Corporation

ALEXANDER CALDER, JR., Chairman, Executive
    Committee
Union Camp Corporation

PHILIP CALDWELL, Senior Managing Director
Shearson Lehman Brothers Inc.

EDWARD W. CARTER, Chairman Emeritus
Carter Hawley Hale Stores, Inc.

EVERETT N. CASE
Van Hornesville, New York

HUNG WO CHING, Chairman of the Board
Aloha Airlines, Inc.

WALKER L. CISLER
Detroit, Michigan

ROBERT C. COSGROVE
Naples, Florida

GEORGE S. CRAFT
Atlanta, Georgia

JOHN P. CUNNINGHAM, Honorary Chairman of the
    Board
Cunningham & Walsh, Inc.

JOHN H. DANIELS, Retired Chairman
National City Bancorporation

ARCHIE K. DAVIS, Chairman of the Board (Retired)
Wachovia Bank and Trust Company, N.A.

DONALD C. DAYTON, Director
Dayton Hudson Corporation

DOUGLAS DILLON, Chairman, Executive Committee
Dillon, Read and Co. Inc.

ALFRED W. EAMES, JR., Retired Chairman
Del Monte Corporation

FRANCIS E. FERGUSON, Retired Chairman
    of the Board
Northwestern Mutual Life Insurance
    Company

JOHN T. FEY, Chairman
The National Westminster Bank USA

WILLIAM S. FISHMAN, Chairman, Executive
    Committee
ARA Services, Inc.

EDMUND FITZGERALD
Milwaukee, Wisconsin

JOHN M. FOX
Orlando, Florida

CLARENCE FRANCIS
New York, New York

GAYLORD FREEMAN
Chicago, Illinois

DON C. FRISBEE, Chairman
PacifiCorp

W. H. KROME GEORGE, Chairman,
    Executive Committee
Aluminum Company of America

PAUL S. GEROT, Honorary Chairman of the
    Board
The Pillsbury Company

LINCOLN GORDON, Guest Scholar
The Brookings Institution

KATHARINE GRAHAM, Chairman
The Washington Post Company

JOHN D. GRAY, Chairman Emeritus
Hartmarx Corp.

WILLIAM C. GREENOUGH, Retired
    Chairman
TIAA and CREF

WALTER A. HAAS, JR., Honorary Chairman
    of the Board
Levi Strauss and Co.

MICHAEL L. HAIDER
New York, New York

TERRANCE HANOLD
Minneapolis, Minnesota

JOHN D. HARPER, Retired Chairman
Aluminum Company of America

ROBERT S. HATFIELD
New York, New York

H. J. HEINZ II, Chairman
H. J. Heinz Company

J. V. HERD, Director
The Continental Insurance Companies

OVETA CULP HOBBY, Chairman
H&C Communications, Inc.

GEORGE F. JAMES
South Bristol, Maine

HENRY R. JOHNSTON
Ponte Vedra Beach, Florida

GILBERT E. JONES, Retired Vice Chairman
IBM Corporation

FREDERICK R. KAPPEL
Sarasota, Florida

CHARLES KELLER, JR.
New Orleans, Louisiana

DAVID M. KENNEDY
Salt Lake City, Utah

JAMES R. KENNEDY
Essex Fells, New Jersey

CHARLES N. KIMBALL, President Emeritus
Midwest Research Institute

HARRY W. KNIGHT, Chairman of the Board
Hillsboro Associates, Inc.

SIGURD S. LARMON
New York, New York

ELMER L. LINDSETH
Shaker Heights, Ohio

JAMES A. LINEN
Greenwich, Connecticut

GEORGE H. LOVE
Pittsburgh, Pennsylvania

ROBERT A. LOVETT, Partner
Brown Brothers Harriman & Co.

ROY G. LUCKS
San Francisco, California

FRANKLIN J. LUNDING
Sarasota, Florida

RAY W. MacDONALD, Honorary Chairman of the
Board
Burroughs Corporation

IAN MacGREGOR, Former Chairman
AMAX Inc.

MALCOLM MacNAUGHTON, Chairman, Executive
Committee
Castle & Cooke, Inc.

FRANK L. MAGEE
Stahlstown, Pennsylvania

G. BARRON MALLORY
New York, New York

STANLEY MARCUS, Consultant
Carter Hawley Hale Stores, Inc.

AUGUSTINE R. MARUSI, Chairman, Executive
Committee
Borden Inc.

OSCAR G. MAYER, Retired Chairman
Oscar Mayer & Co.

L. F. McCOLLUM
Houston, Texas

JOHN A. McCONE
Pebble Beach, California

GEORGE C. McGHEE, Corporate Director
and Former U.S. Ambassador
Washington, D.C.

J.W. McSWINEY, Director
The Mead Corporation

CHAUNCEY J. MEDBERRY III, Chairman, Executive
Committee
Bank of America N.T. & S.A.

JOHN F. MERRIAM
San Francisco, California

LORIMER D. MILTON
Citizens Trust Company

DON G. MITCHELL
Summit, New Jersey

LEE L. MORGAN, Chairman of the Board, Retired
Caterpillar Tractor Co.

ROBERT R. NATHAN, Chairman
Robert R. Nathan Associates, Inc.

ALFRED C. NEAL
Harrison, New York

J. WILSON NEWMAN, Former Chairman of the
Board
Dun & Bradstreet Corporation

AKSEL NIELSEN, Chairman, Finance Committee
Ladd Petroleum Corporation

THOMAS O. PAINE, President
Thomas Paine Associates

JOHN H. PERKINS, Former President
Continental Illinois National Bank and Trust Company
of Chicago

HOWARD C. PETERSEN
Radnor, Pennsylvania

C. WREDE PETERSMEYER
John's Island, Florida

RUDOLPH A. PETERSON, President (Retired)
Bank of America N.T. & S.A.

DONALD C. PLATTEN, Chairman, Executive
Committee
Chemical Bank

R. STEWART RAUCH, Former Chairman
The Philadelphia Saving Fund Society

PHILIP D. REED
New York, New York

AXEL G. ROSIN, Retired Chairman
Book-of-the-Month Club, Inc.

WILLIAM M. ROTH
San Francisco, California

GEORGE RUSSELL
Bloomfield Hills, Michigan

E. C. SAMMONS, Chairman of the Board (Emeritus)
The United States National Bank of Oregon

CHARLES J. SCANLON
Essex, Connecticut

JOHN A. SCHNEIDER, President
Warner Amex Satellite Entertainment Company

ELLERY SEDGWICK, JR.
Cleveland Heights, Ohio

ROBERT B. SEMPLE, Retired Chairman
BASF Wyandotte Corporation

LEON SHIMKIN, Chairman
Simon and Schuster, Inc.

RICHARD R. SHINN, Former Chairman
Metropolitan Life Insurance Company

WILLIAM P. SIMMONS, Chairman
Trust Company of Middle Georgia

NEIL D. SKINNER
Indianapolis, Indiana

ELLIS D. SLATER
Landrum, South Carolina

DONALD B. SMILEY, Chairman, Finance Committee
R. H. Macy & Co., Inc.

DAVIDSON SOMMERS
Washington, D.C.

ROBERT C. SPRAGUE, Honorary Chairman of the
Board
Sprague Electric Company

ELVIS J. STAHR, JR., Partner
Chickering & Gregory

FRANK STANTON, President Emeritus
CBS Inc.

SYDNEY STEIN, JR., Partner
Stein Roe & Farnham

EDGAR B. STERN, JR., President
Royal Street Corporation

J. PAUL STICHT, Chairman, Executive
Committee
R. J. Reynolds Industries, Inc.

ALEXANDER L. STOTT
Ponte Vedra, Florida

C. A. TATUM, JR., Chairman
Texas Utilities Company

ALAN H. TEMPLE
New York, New York

WAYNE E. THOMPSON, Chairman
Merritt Peralta Medical Center

CHARLES C. TILLINGHAST, JR.
Providence, Rhode Island

HOWARD S. TURNER, Retired Chairman
Turner Construction Company

ROBERT C. WEAVER
New York, New York

JAMES E. WEBB
Washington, D.C.

GEORGE WEISSMAN, Chairman, Executive
Committee
Philip Morris Incorporated

WILLIAM H. WENDEL, Vice Chairman
Kennecott Corporation

J. HUBER WETENHALL
New York, New York

GEORGE L. WILCOX, Retired Vice Chairman
Westinghouse Electric Corporation

ARTHUR M. WOOD, Director
Sears, Roebuck and Co.

THEODORE O. YNTEMA
Department of Economics
Oakland University

Honorary Trustees On Leave
For Government Service

WILLIAM A. HEWITT
U.S. Ambassador to Jamaica

RESEARCH ADVISORY BOARD

Chairman
THOMAS C. SCHELLING
Professor of Political Economy
John Fitzgerald Kennedy School of Government
Harvard University

RICHARD N. COOPER
Maurits C. Boas Professor of
    International Economics
Harvard University

MARTIN FELDSTEIN
President
National Bureau of Economic Research, Inc.

VICTOR R. FUCHS
Professor of Economics
Stanford University

DONALD HAIDER
Professor and Program Director
J.L. Kellogg Graduate School of Management
Northwestern University

PAUL KRUGMAN
Professor of Economics
Sloan School of Management
Massachusetts Institute of Technology

PAUL W. McCRACKEN
Edmund Ezra Day University Professor
Graduate School of Business Administration
University of Michigan

JACK A. MEYER
Resident Fellow in Economics
American Enterprise Institute for Public Policy Research

DANIEL H. SAKS
Professor of Education Policy and of Economics
Institute for Public Policy Studies
Vanderbilt University

ISABEL V. SAWHILL
Program Director
The Urban Institute

CHARLES L. SCHULTZE
Senior Fellow
The Brookings Institution

CED PROFESSIONAL AND ADMINISTRATIVE STAFF

ROBERT C. HOLLAND
President

SOL HURWITZ
Senior Vice President and
 Secretary, Board of Trustees

NATHANIEL M. SEMPLE
Vice President,
 Director of Governmental
 Affairs, and Secretary,
 Research and Policy Committee

PATRICIA O'CONNELL
Vice President and
 Director of Finance

FRANK W. SCHIFF
Vice President
 and Chief Economist

R. SCOTT FOSLER
Vice President and
 Director of Government Studies

ELIZABETH J. LUCIER
Comptroller

KENNETH McLENNAN
Vice President and Director
 of Industrial Studies

CLAUDIA P. FEUREY
Vice President and
 Director of Information

*Advisor on International
Economic Policy*

ISAIAH FRANK
William L. Clayton Professor of
 International Economics
 The Johns Hopkins University

Research
SEONG H. PARK
Economist

LORRAINE M. BROOKER
Economic Research Associate

Governmental Affairs
PEGGY MORRISSETTE
Deputy Director
 and Deputy Secretary,
 Research and Policy Committee

Conferences
RUTH MUNSON
Manager

Accounting
CATHERINE F. LEAHY
Deputy Comptroller

Information and Publications
HECTOR GUENTHER
Deputy Director

SANDRA KESSLER HAMBURG
Assistant Director

DEBRA H. KANFER
Publications Manager

Finance
RUTH KALLA
Deputy Director

DOUGLAS A. STAPLES
Associate Director

AMY JEAN O'NEILL
Campaign Coordinator

Administration
THEODORA BOSKOVIC
Administrative Assistant
 to the President

SHIRLEY R. SHERMAN
Administrative Assistant
 to the President

JOHN SULLIVAN WILSON
Assistant to the President

BETTY S. TRIMBLE
Assistant Office Manager

Information Services
TIMOTHY J. MUENCH
Manager

STATEMENTS ON NATIONAL POLICY
ISSUED BY THE RESEARCH AND POLICY COMMITTEE

More Effective Programs for a Cleaner Environment *(1974)*

The Management and Financing of Colleges *(1973)*

Strengthening the World Monetary System *(1973)*

Financing the Nation's Housing Needs *(1973)*

Building a National Health-Care System *(1973)*

*A New Trade Policy Toward Communist Countries *(1972)*

High Employment Without Inflation:
  A Positive Program for Economic Stabilization *(1972)*

Reducing Crime and Assuring Justice *(1972)*

Military Manpower and National Security *(1972)*

The United States and the European Community:
  Policies for a Changing World Economy *(1971)*

Improving Federal Program Performance *(1971)*

Social Responsibilities of Business Corporations *(1971)*

Education for the Urban Disadvantaged:
  From Preschool to Employment *(1971)*

Further Weapons Against Inflation *(1970)*

Making Congress More Effective *(1970)*

Training and Jobs for the Urban Poor *(1970)*

Improving the Public Welfare System *(1970)*

Reshaping Government in Metropolitan Areas *(1970)*

Economic Growth in the United States *(1969)*

Assisting Development in Low-Income Countries *(1969)*

*Nontariff Distortions of Trade *(1969)*

Fiscal and Monetary Policies for Steady Economic Growth *(1969)*

Financing a Better Election System *(1968)*

Innovation in Education: New Directions for the American School *(1968)*

Modernizing State Government *(1967)*

*Trade Policy Toward Low-Income Countries *(1967)*

How Low Income Countries Can Advance Their Own Growth *(1966)*

Modernizing Local Government *(1966)*

Budgeting for National Objectives *(1966)*

*Statements issued in association with CED counterpart organizations in foreign countries.

CED COUNTERPART ORGANIZATIONS
IN FOREIGN COUNTRIES

Close relations exist between the Committee for Economic Development and independent, nonpolitical research organizations in other countries. Such counterpart groups are composed of business executives and scholars and have objectives similar to those of CED, which they pursue by similarly objective methods. CED cooperates with these organizations on research and study projects of common interest to the various countries concerned. This program has resulted in a number of joint policy statements involving such international matters as energy, East-West trade, assistance to the developing countries, and the reduction of nontariff barriers to trade.

CE	Círculo de Empresarios Serrano Jover 5-2°, Madrid 8, Spain
CEDA	Committee for Economic Development of Australia 139 Macquarie Street, Sydney 2001, New South Wales, Australia
CEPES	Europäische Vereinigung für Wirtschaftliche und Soziale Entwicklung Reuterweg 14,6000 Frankfurt/Main, West Germany
IDEP	Institut de l'Entreprise 6, rue Clément-Marot, 75008 Paris, France
経済同友会	Keizai Doyukai (Japan Committee for Economic Development) Japan Industrial Club Bldg. 1 Marunouchi, Chiyoda-ku, Tokyo, Japan
PSI	Policy Studies Institute 100, Park Village East, London NW1 3SR, England
SNS	Studieförbundet Näringsliv och Samhälle Sköldungagatan 2, 11427 Stockholm, Sweden